Irish Crafts & Craftsmen

IRISH CRAFTS & CRAFTSMEN

JOHN MANNERS

Appletree Press

First published in 1982 and printed by
The Appletree Press Ltd
7 James St South
Belfast BT2 8DL

British Library Cataloguing in Publication Data
Manners, John
  Irish crafts and craftsmen.
  1. Handicraft—Ireland
  I. Title
  680'.9415   TT59

ISBN 0-904651-92-4

CONTENTS

CRAFTS LOCATION MAP

Places mentioned throughout the book only have been included; thatching, stone-walling, smithery and farriery, which are widely practised throughout the country, have been omitted.

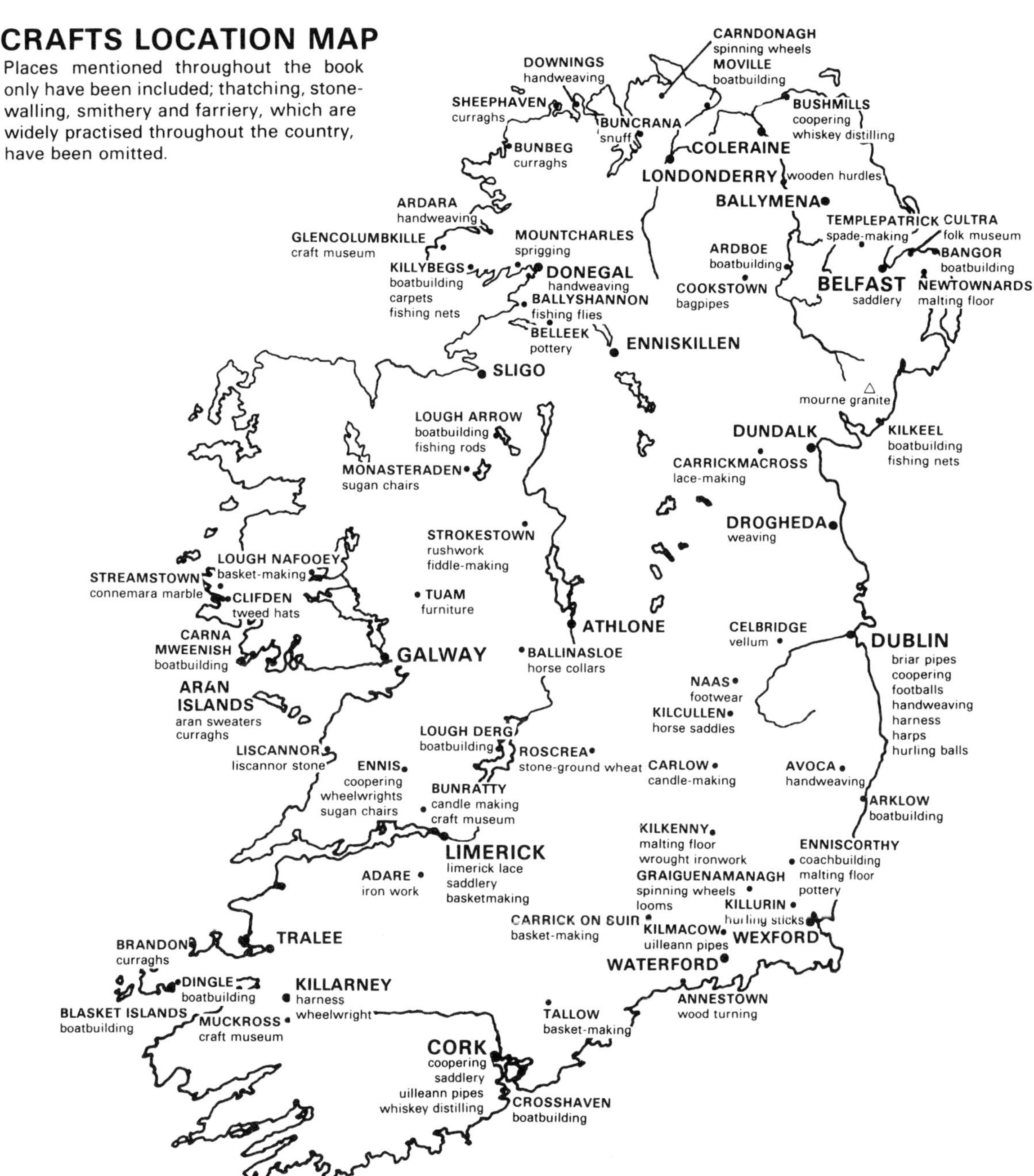

ACKNOWLEDGMENTS

Many individuals helped me locate the craftsmen, in particular Miss Blanaid Reddin of Bord Fáilte, Miss Muriel Gahan of Dublin, Mrs Duignan of the Slieve Bawn Cooperative, Strokestown, and G. B. Thompson, Director of the Ulster Folk and Transport Museum, Cultra, Co. Down.

I would also like to record the assistance received from all the craftsmen I visited who, without exception, were helpful and allowed photographs to be taken. They are all proud of their work, even if their skills do not as a rule bring them the material riches they deserve.

FOREWORD

The aim of this book is to present, in words and photographs, a general picture of the state of crafts and craftsmen in Ireland at the present time. While it is well known that a number of traditional crafts have been in decline for years, yet it is remarkable how many have survived, even if, as a rule, their end-products do not find their way into the stores of our cities and towns. Yet, while many, such as thatching, saddlery, farriery, boatbuilding and coopering (the making of barrels) fulfil an essential local need, others such as hand-weaving and Aran knitting, are able to compete in wider, international markets.

Traditionally, the craftsman's particular skill has been passed down from father to son. Several included here represent the fifth generation of a family business. If a man's father did not practice a craft, it would therefore be difficult for him to acquire one, for craftsmen were wary of competition, and on those occasions when apprentices were engaged, they had to pay for the privilege.

However, the Irish scene has been changing. There is more prosperity in rural areas, and new factories are being built which provide regular wages and good working conditions, both of which tend to draw workers away from the rural districts where crafts are still practiced and profit margins arc low. At the same time there are an increasing number of craft shops catering for the tourist trade and they provide excellent outlets for articles such as Aran sweaters, hand-woven goods and rush and willow baskets.

The recent revival in interest in crafts of all kinds has given rise to the publication of excellent booklets by Bord Fáilte in Dublin and the Local Enterprise Development Unit in Belfast. These list places where craftsmen and women sell their products and where they can often be seen at work. The accent here is mostly on so-called 'artist' crafts. The traditional craftsman produces little or no surplus to sell, as he generally only makes enough to satisfy the needs of the local community, surviving both by goodwill and a reputation built up over generations.

1
WOOD WORKERS

Ireland has fewer trees than anywhere else in Europe, though with ample supplies of peat much of it has escaped being used for firewood. With communities spread out and communications poor, each locality in the past became largely self-supporting, and requirements like furniture were roughly fashioned by the local handyman.

Native trees consist mainly of the hardwoods of oak, ash, beech and a little elm, and the softwoods almost entirely of larch.

Sugan Chairs

There is very little tradition of furniture-making in Ireland. Furniture throughout Europe was scarce and spartan until the 17th century when it became increasingly comfortable, though by this time many Irish trees had been cut down, particularly the oak, and all wood was scarce. A certain amount of use was made of bog oak which was hard and thus difficult to work.

One type of truly native furniture made by local craftsmen is the

A sugan chair.

14

sugan chair with its straw seat. They are turned out by John Kelly of Kinturk Homecraft near Ennis in Co. Clare, a co-operative with a substantial output and also, amongst others, by Jim Kett near Adare, Co. Limerick. The latter was originally a wheelwright but when tractors and trailors became widely available, he turned to making furniture.

Beech is commonly used for the frames and the pieces are cut to shape with a band saw. Sugan means straw and originally all chairs had seats of this or of hay. First a rope is made by twisting straw using an old-style straw hook or a cranked-handle rope twister. Any straw can be used though in practice this is usually of oat or wheat as these are the most readily available. The seat is made by threading the straw across, then up and down, and finally by winding it round several times from back to front, giving it a neat finish and hiding the work underneath. Nowadays thin sisal rope is widely used and it takes about half an hour to seat each chair, though the finished article may lack the rustic appearance of the traditional straw seat.

The chairs vary in style, some being fitted with slatted backs, others with vertical strutted backs, while a few are built as rocking chairs. John Kett makes reproduction cock-fighting chairs, in which spectators sit back-to-front with their arms resting on the top of the back of the chairs.

Another well-known chairmaker is John Surlis of Monasteraden, Co. Roscommon, now aged 79, and the seventh generation of woodworkers and coopers. He works on his own and is a craftsman of the old school, turning out each piece individually by hand. He has seen many changes from the time he made wooden churns, butter firkins, tool handles, barrows, pig troughs and anything else of wood including wheelwrighting, and proudly displays a certificate for work selected for the first World Crafts Exhibition in Toronto in 1974 when his chair was one of the two Irish exhibits. He works mostly with ash which he used to cut himself and season

 *John Surlis of Monasteraden, Co. Roscommon, using a draw knife to make a chair leg.*

for two years before use, though he now buys it, complaining that all the best wood has been cut down since the introduction of the chain saw. His workshop is a museum: he sits at his 'grey mare' with a foot brake that firmly clamps the wood, while he deftly fashions it into shape using a draw knife. His staple products are kitchen chairs which he calls 'Leitrim chairs', being a native of that county, and a number of his exhibits are on display in the Dublin Museum.

Al O'Dea of Tuam, Co. Galway, the founder of Corrib Crafts.

A more recent and very successful firm is 'Corrib Crafts' of Tuam, Co. Galway, founded fifteen years ago by Al O'Dea. Here the accent is on top quality workmanship and materials, with the work being carried out in kiln dried Iroko, a wood similar to teak which comes

from Nigeria. Individual pieces are usually morticed and tenoned, and held together with pegs and dowels, using very little glue. The completed articles are then given a linseed oil finish. The designs are simple and without frills which, together with their high quality, make them very attractive in appearance. One feature of the twenty-strong work force is their youth; all have been recruited

In the workshops of Al O'Dea at Tuam.

18

locally and make an enthusiastic and efficient team. They make sugan chairs, tables, cots, corner cupboards and fit out churches, bars, and hotels as well as goods for export.

Spinning Wheels

There are many variations in the design of spinning wheels which were brought to Ireland by refugees and traders, one of the earliest being the Earl of Strafford, who set up an industry near Belfast in the seventeenth century for the spinning of flax. The oldest and simplest wheels consisted of a large diameter wheel that was

John Shiel making a spinning wheel at Carndonagh, Co. Donegal.

turned by hand. A string around the circumference rotated a spindle held horizontally in position by bands of straw at each end. The more usual wheel is the horizontal type worked by foot, where the wool or flax goes through a hole in the spindle, and is threaded to a flier which feeds it onto a bobbin. One of the finest collections in the world can be seen at the Ulster Folk Museum at Cultra, Co. Down.

There is a steady demand for new wheels today, and they are turned out in reasonable numbers by John Shiel of Carndonagh, Co. Donegal, assisted by his son; they make about four of the Donegal flax-type of wheel per week, using mahogany. The work involves wood turning and the making of metal parts. Another maker is Edward Cahill of Graiguenamanagh, Co. Kilkenny, who also makes Donegal-type wheels in mahogany. His wheels are turned out singly and are made to a high degree of precision; they may well become the antiques of tomorrow.

Looms

As weavers need good light to work by, their cottages would have had larger windows than usual, and their dwellings thus specially built for them. The weavers were likely farmers who operated their looms during slack periods, particularly in the winter.

Hand weaving using wooden looms is carried out on a moderate scale in Co. Donegal. It is still possible to make a living out of it and other handloom weavers include the Avoca Weavers of Co. Wicklow and the Weavers Shed in Dublin, as well as a few individuals dotted about the country, usually near the main tourist centres. However, hand weaving has steadily decreased and there are probably a large number of unused looms hidden away in cottages in more remote areas.

Edward Cahill of Graiguenamanagh, Co. Kilkenny, makes them

to order, producing looms of a very high standard using the best available materials. Cahill started production in 1971 and has built up a flourishing business; his two sons have since joined him to cope with demand. Normally looms are between forty-eight and seventy-two inches wide but one he built for Avoca Weavers was 134 inches in width in order to make 'king-size' bedspreads for the American market. Looms used to be made with any available wood, properly seasoned, while mostly deal is used now, with teak or mahogany for the more expensive models. The work is beautifully executed, dovetailed and held together with wedges so that it can be dismantled with ease; a seventy-two inch loom can be put on the roof rack of a car, an important consideration as they are very bulky when set up.

Turning

Wood turning is usually combined with making articles such as spinning wheel spokes and chair legs, and in recent years a number of artist craftsmen have set up in business.

They produce mostly small articles, chiefly for the tourist trade, using imported as well as home grown wood. Of the latter, suitable woods for turning are yew, elm, ash, beech, sycamore and, more rarely, bog oak. At Waterford Woodcraft Ltd, of Annestown, Co. Waterford, an Australian, Bruce McDonald, and Heather Mitchell, who thinks she is the only lady woodworker in the country, produce a range of attractive and useful objects which are sold in the adjoining shop.

2
BOAT BUILDERS

Large Fishing Boats

The building of fishing boats has long been an important industry, and Irish yards are able to build wooden boats from sixty to eighty-six feet in length, the largest economical size. Almost all these larger wooden vessels are built for fishing; they carry a crew of about eight, stay at sea for two or three days' fishing for herring and white fish and, almost without exception, are privately owned.

Wooden construction calls for fine craftmanship, particularly in the making of the curved frames for the hull, shaping the bows and making the keel. Most Irish yards have been in business a long time and employ a high percentage of long serving and experienced craftsmen. All use Irish oak for the frames or ribs. Some cut the trunks into thick planks when the wood first arrives, allowing for some seasoning. The curved ribs are then cut to shape and made into several sections which are bolted together. In the past the side planking was normally of larch but supplies of good quality Irish larch are not now readily obtained and there has been a swing to imported iroko, much more expensive and heavier, but as a

Repairing a Galway Bay lugger.

hardwood it gives better service, is very good for deck planking, and comes in longer lengths which minimise joins. Wood side-planking has to be trimmed to shape and then steamed to make it pliable, the lengths of the planks varying as the joins must not be directly one above another. The planks are then secured in place by a mixture of bolts and large galvanised nails.

The longest wooden fishing boat in service used to be one of eighty-two feet in length, built at Downings, Co. Donegal. This has since been overtaken by two of eighty-six feet, built at the BIM yard at Killybegs, Co. Donegal, the largest wooden-boat builders in Ireland. Occasionally there is an order for an ususual boat; one such vessel was the *St Brendan,* built to an ancient design with a thirty-six feet long frame made of oak and ash, without a keel, and with the outside covered with forty-nine ox hides stitched together and sails of the same material. This vessel crossed the Atlantic, following in the steps of St Brendan's journey in the sixth century, and was made by men at the Crosshaven Boatyard near Cork, who also made the *Gipsy Moth V,* in which Sir Francis Chichester sailed round the world. Although this yard makes fishing vessels it concentrates on wooden yachts, using laminated wood. Half the work is of new construction and half refitting, a ratio that applies to nearly all yards. Some lifeboats are also refitted here, although many more are overhauled at Bangor Shipyards, Co. Down.

Around the coast a number of smaller yards make boats thirty-six feet in length or less. Some of these smaller yards are very long established and two of them, McDonalds of Moville, Co. Donegal, and Clohertys of Mweenish, Co. Galway, have both been in business over two hundred years, and six generations. Mark Cloherty is a craftsman of the old school who still shapes his wood with an adze, using methods practised over centuries. He specialises in carvel-built boats, solid and strong vessels that have a life expectancy of about forty years, and which can be fitted with outboard motors; they are mainly used for lobster and line fishing.

Mark Cloherty, boatbuilder, of Mweenish, Co. Galway, shaping a piece of wood using an adze.

All the larger boats are carvel built, i.e. with side-planking lying side by side to give a smooth finish, as opposed to being clinker built, i.e. where the planks overlap each other. The sterns of nearly all fishing vessels are of the transom design, giving them a square shaped stern, the exceptions being mostly around north Donegal, where cruiser, or rounded sterns are more normal.

Lake and River Boats

With so many lakes and rivers there is a large demand for boats for fishing, pleasure and cruising, and here the traditional boatbuilders are faced with the challenge of fibreglass craft. Nearly all the pleasure motor cruisers and a number of the smaller fishing boats are made out of fibreglass now, its chief advantage being that less maintainance is required and annual re-painting is unnecessary. Traditionalists claim that fibreglass boats skate about the surface of the water in windy conditions; in any case, these boats have most of their internal fittings made of wood and they also require a lot of joinery work.

A few individual builders are left who use traditional methods, among them John Tuohy on Lough Derg, Co. Clare and Peter Quigley, who trained under Walter Levigne of Athlone. Their boats have oak ribs and keels with larch side-planking, are clinker built and held together with copper rivets. One individual can build about fifteen boats a year and, with an assistant, can turn out one per week, though demand rarely requires this. Builders are currently concerned about the quality of the larch, which, while it does not rot, can split; knots in the wood, however, can minimise this and are used to advantage. Oars are made from white spruce or a similar wood and are fashioned from planks ten feet in length, cut to shape and given a curve to the blade.

A completely different type of boat is used by the eel fishermen

John Tuohy of Loch Derg, Co. Clare, a well-known builder of boats.

on Lough Neagh. These are about twenty-five feet in length, clinker built with a high freeboard, and fitted with an engine. There are about 170 licenced boats and a small but steady demand for replacements. Charlie McIlroy of Ardboe is the only traditional

boatbuilder left here. His boats are built with oak frames, with side-planking of larch, mahogany or iroko, although here again fibreglass has made its appearance. Boats are now built from a mould taken from one of his own boats, without royalties or compensation being paid.

Curraghs

Curraghs are still in use, though on a decreasing scale, on the west coast from Donegal to Kerry, varying is size from about sixteen feet in length and rowed by one man, to the larger ones of double that size. They were originally made with frames of willow sallies or hazel and longitudinal laths of some suitable cleft wood with an oak gunwhale, the whole being covered with hide and tied

Carrying a curragh up the beach at Inisheer, Aran Islands.

together with horsehair. The modern version is used for carrying passengers, fishing, collecting kelp and, in the smaller Aran Islands, for transporting cargo from ship to shore. Their main virtue is ease of building, coupled with extreme lightness enabling them to ride easily in heavy seas. There is no keel and the bottom is built on a curve with a characteristic pointed bow that slopes sharply upwards. Their life is around twenty years, although demand is such that making them is not now a full-time occupation.

Many different woods are used in their construction, the best gunwhales being of oak, though white deal is frequently used now. A large curragh at Inisheer has oak ribs, others larch, while a small

John Goodwin of Maharees, Dingle, making one of his last curraghs.

The framework of a curragh being made in the Aran Islands.

one at Sheephaven in north Donegal has hazel ribs tied to the lengthwise laths; John Goodwin of Dingle, Co. Kerry, is now using parana pine. The latter is probably the best known curragh maker and advised on the building of the *St Brendan*. He reckons that he has built about two hundred curraghs in his time, though now aged eighty-three, he plans to retire shortly.

Another interesting builder is Tom Daly from the Blasket Islands, about three miles off the Dingle peninsula, which was evacuated some years ago. As there was no bull on the islands cows had to be brought to the mainland to be served. Their legs were tied and they were lifted into the curragh, although as the cow

32

'sometimes made the curragh a bit giddy' a second vessel accompanied it as a precaution in case of accident. In the smaller Aran Islands cattle are still 'swum' from ship to shore behind the curragh.

In building a curragh the gunwhale is made first, and the ribs fitted into slots cut in it. The ribs will first have been cut to an exact length and made pliable for steaming; the simplest form of steamer is a length of cast iron pipe blocked at one end and partially filled with water. The ribs are put in this and the pipe is then placed over a fire of waste chippings and boiled for a short time. They have to be fitted quickly in order to retain their pliability so they are placed over a former of the required curvature until needed. After they have been fitted in the gunwhale laths are secured on the outside and the cover then hand- or machine-stitched onto the frame. This skin is finally treated with hot pitch which gives the curragh its black appearance. Oars are made from deal with a very narrow blade. At the inboard end near the loom is a piece of wood called a boll. This has a hole in it that fits over a thole pin in the gunwhale and holds it in position.

3 STONE WORKERS

While most quarries now produce stone for the construction of new roads and improving existing ones, there remains a handful of quarries producing stone for pavings and building, etc. Liscannor stone and Connemara marble come into this category, both quarries having been reopened about fifteen years ago, while Mourne granite has been quarried continuously for many years.

Liscannor Stone

Liscannor stone comes from the north of County Clare and is quarried near the Cliffs of Moher. Being situated near the sea enabled the stone to be transported by ship, and at the turn of the century was quarried on a large scale, much of it for export. Geologically the stone is close-grained, blue grey sandstone of the millstone grit and flagstone series of the carboniferous period, very hard and resistant to acid. It splits quite easily into large blocks from one to six inches in thickness and the large pieces can be squared by hand or cut with a diamond saw. It is ideal for paving stones, flooring or facing stone on buildings, with an attractive blue

grey appearance and a slightly rough surface. Locally it is used as roofing material and is laid like slate. Its use and the way it splits is very similar to that produced in the north of Scotland and called 'Cathness slabs'.

The workforce at Liscannor consists of fifteen men who work two

Splitting a slab of Liscannor stone.

36

quarries, in one of which the stone splits naturally thinner than the other. It lies in a horizontal bed and is of such flatness that it looks as if it has been produced artificially. Extraction is by the careful insertion of wedges around the edges. Two levers are inserted at one end and gently prised up and a sheet of stone is raised. The far edge is struck a number of times with a heavy hammer and the sheet then becomes detached and ready for dressing. If intended as a cladding stone for a building, it is hand dressed by squaring and trimming with a hammer. The capacity of the Irish market to absorb all the stone is rather limited and much is exported. In England it can be seen in, among other places, the Royal Mint and St John's Tower in the Tower of London.

Connemara Marble

The only marble produced in Ireland comes from Connemara. It is highly marked and has an attractive appearance in tones of rich green, brown, silver grey and white. Geologically it is one of the oldest orders of rock, being from the pre-Cambrian period, which gives it an age of about 700 million years. It is obtained from one small quarry at Streamstown, Co. Galway, which was worked irregularly prior to 1965, when Lord Mayo, talking to a friend, remarked that it might be a good move if the quarry was started up again; the latter replied that he thought the idea a good one and why did he not do it himself? Terence Bourke, the tenth Earl of Mayo, a versatile ex-Royal Navy pilot with an inventive turn of mind, accepted the challenge and brought the quarry into production in 1965. He perfected and patented a number of processes including a saw to cut veneers of marble and a method of backing it. This, coupled with the construction of a new factory in 1975, led quickly to success.

Supplies of marble are good, with plenty of reserves, and the method of extraction is noteworthy. The marble is cut by an

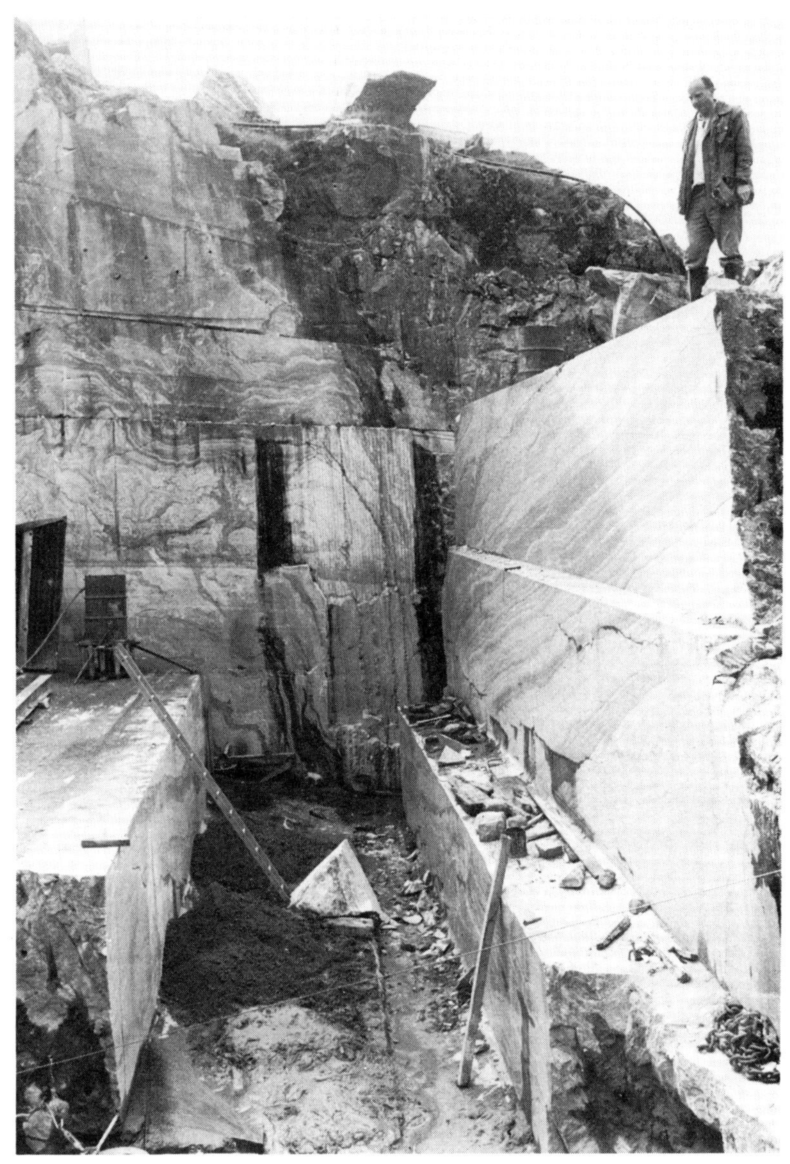

Lord Mayo at his Connemara marble quarry at Streamstown, Co. Galway.

ordinary mild steel wire fed with silica sand and lubricated with water. The hard silica slowly saws through the marble as the wire is drawn along it. Long blocks about thirty feet long, six feet high and three feet deep are cut. Each block is levered onto its side, cushioning itself on the soft sandy waste. It is then examined for flaws, and when passed large chunks are hoisted by crane, ready for cutting into workable sizes. Lord Mayo's patents enable four millimetre thick veneers to be produced and these are further reduced to three millimetres by grinding and polishing. His latest saw, with hardened steel tips impregnated with industrial diamonds, is able to cut pieces ten feet by four, which are suitable for table tops or small wall panels. These veneers are mounted on a kind of rigid honeycomb backing and are the only marble veneers in the world. The sheets can be cut to make attractive designs and to produce smaller items like chess and backgammon boards. The marble is hard, wears well, and is resistant to staining; it therefore makes attractive flooring material and has recently been laid in Galway Cathedral.

Mourne Granite

The area around the foot of the Mourne Mountains in Co. Down is famous for its granite and, being close to the sea, the finished products could be transported by ship. The hard granite that was produced was excellent for making kerbs and stone setts, entailing intensive labour in shaping the stone, but compensated for by its durability. This work finally ceased about nine years ago after dwindling over the years. Stone setts are no longer wanted, while kerbs are universally made of concrete; they are easy to produce but unattractive in appearance. The area produced generations of stone masons and, as local granite decreased, the stone industry turned to imported stone. The shaping calls for machine operators rather than stonemasons, as it is cut by diamond saws and polished with carborundum. Some of the older men are still skilled stonemasons but their craftsmanship is rarely needed now and is slowly dying in the district.

Dry-Stone Walling

There must be more stone walls in Ireland than anywhere else in the world. They are the best way to enclose a field and fortunately in most places there is an ample supply of stones. Hedges are few and there is a scarcity of wood to make fencing stakes. The walls, frequently called ditches, are invariably built 'dry', meaning that mortar is not used to bind the stones together. Their form and construction vary greatly in detail, depending on the supply and configuration of the stones. While there are a few examples of precision built walls with flat-sided stones, notably in the Liscannor area, stones are not normally of very convenient shapes, either being smooth and round or very irregular. If the supply is insufficient to build a solid stone wall they may be used as a facing to an earth bank. Where there is a surplus, walls may be thick and made from stones picked out of the fields, which would otherwise hamper the smooth working of a plough. They are most dense in the Aran Islands where the tiny fields are enclosed with massive walls which have no gates. A section of the wall has to be taken down and then rebuilt for the entry of an animal while islanders climb over the walls if they want to get into their fields.

While most walls are looked after by farmers, local authority builders also maintain, rebuild and erect new ones. One such expert builder is Enda Moroney, who works in the Ennis district in Co. Clare, and who describes how he builds them. First he removes about two inches of topsoil, or digs down until a good foundation is reached, then places a template in position. Old stone is used when available, supplemented by freshly quarried material if necessary. The larger stones are placed on the outside faces of the

Stone walls on Inishmore, Aran Islands.

40

wall leaving a gap in the middle which is filled with smaller stones. Sometimes in the Ennis area the wall is cemented inside to a height of eighteen inches. This does not show and, though a practice that might displease the purists, gives the wall an added firmness. The top is finished with larger and heavier capping stones, selected for their size and flatness which, if possible, overlap the sides of the wall to help protect it against the elements. These stones are alternated with others laid vertically, giving the wall a castellated effect. Alternately the walls may be capped solely with stones laid vertically on end, and here again the tops are sometimes cemented. The cement is visible and is a feature that many people dislike, but it does hold the stones in position and stops them being dislodged.

4
LEATHER WORKERS

The main users of leather are the saddlery and footwear trades, the former being divided into three separate specialist crafts: those making horse saddles, horse-collars and harnesses. The traditional Irish love of horses for racing, hunting, show jumping, and pony trekking, together with the numerous stud farms, means that there is a good trade for saddlers, although harnesses and horse-collars are not now in great demand. While the initial cost of saddlery is high due to the expense of the leather and the relative slowness and care taken with the hand stitching, if well looked after the saddlers products last a very long time and usually appreciate in value as the cost of labour and material increases.

Harness

Every draught horse needs a set of harness and, while all types of saddlers can deal with the stitching and making of harness, the tendency has been for saddlers to specialise in this type of work, provided demand is sufficient. There has been a renewal of interest in exhibiting carriages and carts in the show ring, creating a steady

demand for new equipment at a time when this kind of business had almost disappeared, and those that have survived are once again doing good business. One such craftsman is Sam Greer of Poolbeg in Dublin, who is fortunate in having his son to help him and carry on the trade. Another concentrating on essential harness work in Killarney, with its jaunting cars, is John Grady who also repairs collars. Most of his work is refitting, though he also makes

John Grady in his saddlery workshop in Killarney.

some new gear. Now aged seventy-three, there will be a big gap when he retires as there should be somebody on the spot, particularly in summer, to maintain the jaunting cars.

Horse-Collars

Demand for horse collars is small but important. There are a sizeable number of horse-drawn vehicles such as jaunting cars, particularly around Killarney, in some larger towns, and on Inishmore in the Aran Islands, all of which cater principally for the tourist trade. There is also a steady increase in the number of horse-drawn caravans for holidaymakers, while other horse-drawn carts are used for transporting milk, peat and working the land. Collars last a long time, but the stitching periodically needs renewing, the serge lining wears out, and they need re-stuffing from time to time with best wool flock.

Rory Kilduff of Ballinasloe, Co. Galway, is probably the only full-time collar maker left in Ireland, and collars are sent to him for repair from all over the country. His business has been in the same house for 280 years and in the same family for over ninety years. There were eleven workers in 1938 but today Rory Kilduff is the only remaining craftsman.

Irish collars differ in design from the British pattern in that they have a strap at the top. To place the collar on a horse the straps are undone, the collar top opened up and placed over the neck, and the straps re-fastened. The other pattern of collar, not nearly so common, has no straps and so does not open; to put it on, the collar is placed over the horse's head upside down and then turned round. In either case there has to be room so the collar does not press on the windpipe. For a new collar, the first part made is the leather wale, which is tubular in cross section, filled with rye straw, and pressed in tight with a stuffing iron. This is attached to the main body which is of leather, with serge lining filled with straw and

Rory Kilduff of Ballinasloe, Co. Galway, one of the few remaining horse-collar makers.

wool flock. The hames, which are fitted with tug hooks, are brought ready-made and fit between the collar and the wale.

Saddles

The saddle-making trade has had fluctuating fortunes throughout this century. With the advent of the motor car, horse-riding declined dramatically though during the past twenty years the market has improved with more racing and leisure riding, and an increase in the popularity of pony trekking. This has led to saddlers enjoying a degree of prosperity, though they are still cautious about the future, for the number of master saddlers is comparatively small and the majority of them are elderly.

The largest and one of the longest-established saddlers is the well-known firm of Berney Brothers of Kilcullen, Co. Kildare, in the heart of racing country. The firm has been in existence since before 1850 and today Thomas Berney, eighty-three years of age, still works at his bench with his two sons and a number of younger workers. Here there are 10 employees, a large number in the saddlery business. Slightly smaller in size is Joseph Gordon, of Belfast, who serves a very large area, while Tom Wallace of Limerick has another flourishing business. Other saddlerys are sparsely spread over the country and in general are small, though necessary concerns. For the most part they concentrate on repairs and selling saddles and equipment bought from Walsall in England, where there are a number of firms dealing in saddlery, tools, horse brasses, etc. Practically all saddlery leather is imported, much of it also coming from the specialist firm of Richardsons of Derby in England, who are world famous for their products.

A large part of a saddlery business involves repair work, which is slow and expensive. The article to be stitched is held in a clamp that is pressed tight with the knees. Two needles and thread are used and pushed through the holes in opposite directions and then pulled tight. The threads are made up by the saddlers from flax rolled against the thigh till of a sufficient thickness and then drawn across a piece of beeswax. Important pieces like stirrup leathers must be of the very best quality and workmanship because a broken strap could cause a serious accident. Apart from renewing stitching, saddles also need periodical re-stuffing with best wool flock, and the serge undersides occasionally need to be replaced.

Berney Brothers do some exporting but in general saddlers are kept too busy supplying the home market and have neither the time nor capacity to export. They sell their saddles direct to the

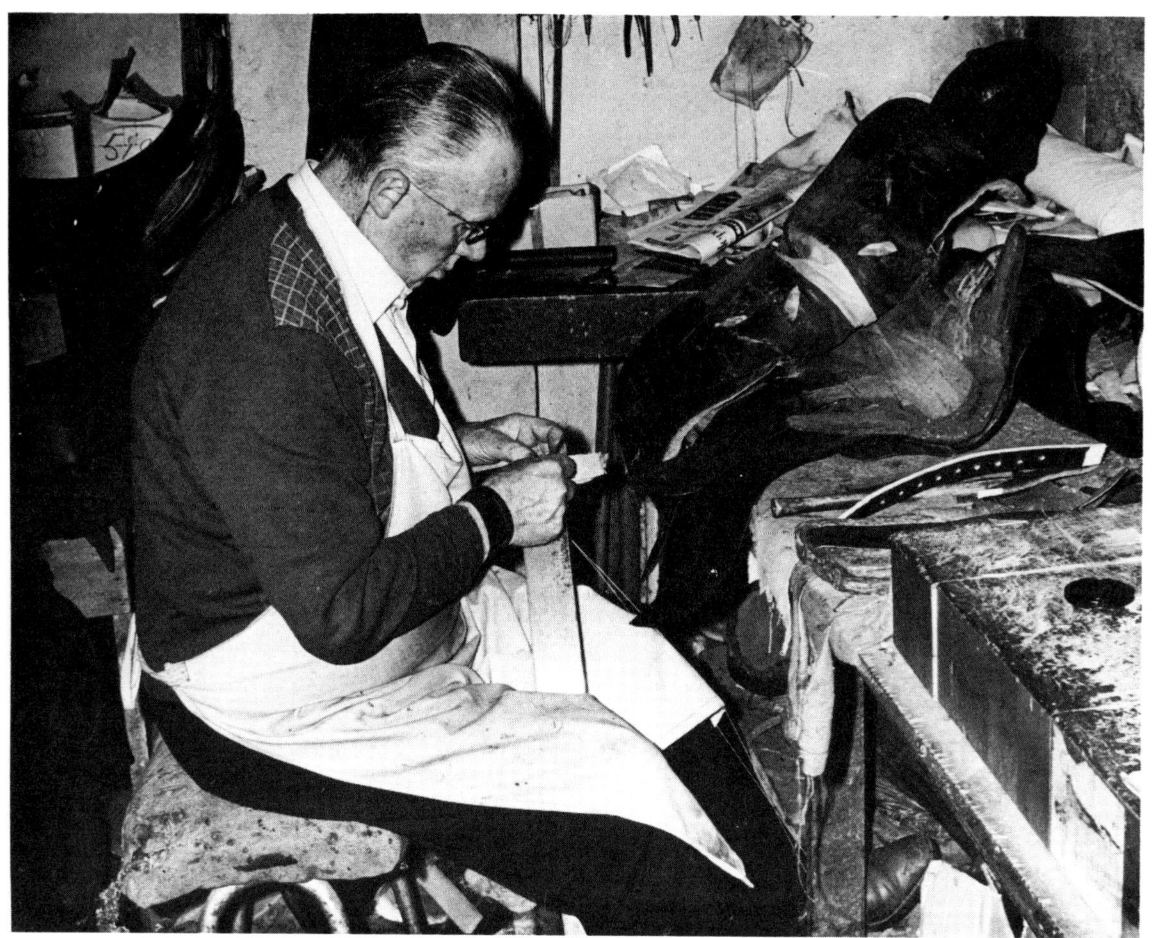

customer, but such is the pressure of work that he or she may have to wait a year for a new saddle. Moreover, as some of the smaller saddlers retire their businesses will close and there will be an inevitable reduction in the number of saddlery shops in the future.

Thomas Berney repairing a saddle at Kilcullen, Co. Kildare.

Footwear

One business still producing hand-made footwear is George Tutty's at Naas, Co. Kildare. At the job for fifty years, he says he is still learning, although while the workforce numbers six, including his son, young people are now reluctant to follow the trade. The footwear is mostly orthopaedic or surgical and, when time permits, shoes are also made for old customers at prices ranging from £40 to £120. The advantages of hand-made shoes are that they fit properly—both feet are measured and it is surprising how few people have feet the same size; secondly, the soles are hand-stitched using nylon thread, which is better and longer lasting than machine stitching; and thirdly, only top quality leather is used. If carefully looked after, shoes and riding boots last a very long time, are a good investment and not all that expensive in the long run as they will outlast several pairs of cheaper products.

As a rule the uppers are machine-stitched but the rest is done by hand and some of the shoes are welted, probably the best way of attaching the sole to the upper and, at the same time, giving the shoe a degree of watertightness. All leather breathes, even after it has been tanned, and it is this quality that has enabled it to keep its supremacy, while millions of pounds have been spent and lost in unsuccessful endeavours to find an acceptable substitute. Such is the demand for George Tutty's footwear that he has to turn away work, showing that there is a strong demand in an exclusive market, but the likelihood is that his business will shrink in spite of demand, due to the lack of new recruits to the trade.

Parchment and Vellum

This is produced on a small scale by the firm of Elzas and Zonen of Celbridge, Co. Kildare. Parchment comes from sheep and goats, and vellum from calves. Both are made by removing the hair, after loosening it with the aid of chemicals, then stretching out the skins on frames to dry. When dry they are scraped down to the membrane, leaving a smooth surface for writing. In the past most documents were written on either parchment or vellum, including illuminated manuscripts, proving that the material lasts a very long time and remains in good condition. Much of the production is now exported and is in demand for presentation diplomas and book coverings, while some goes to make bodhrans (see ch. 10).

5 BLACK SMITHS

The blacksmith was an essential member of any rural community, particularly where transport was poor. From his raw materials he was capable of making almost anything and the articles he made and repaired included farm implements and tools, waggon fittings, gates, spades, turf-cutting slanes, water pumps, shepherd's crooks and, of course, horse-shoes. During this century the blacksmiths' trade has been badly hit by mass-produced farm equipment. This, coupled with a reduction in the horse population on farms, has resulted in far less work for the blacksmith, and many have slowly been squeezed out of business. Blacksmiths have since had to adapt themselves to modern conditions; wrought iron is no longer produced, having become a victim of modern smelting processes, so almost all work is done in mild steel. Every smithy has a coal-fired forge in which the metal is heated. At the side of the forge is a blower to stimulate the fire with its draught, and although the older blacksmiths often use large leather bellows operated by the left hand, these are being replaced by electric bellows. In front of the forge there is always a water trough for cooling the tools or tempering the work. The centrepiece of the smithy is the anvil mounted on a large block of wood that gives it bounce when using a hammer. The anvil has a flat face on top, with a number of holes to take tools like swages and scroll formers and at one end is the beak for fashioning curved pieces of metal such as horse-shoes.

Some of the more progressive craftsmen have specialised in making garden furniture, for which there is an increasing demand. One such firm is the Adare Iron Works in Co. Limerick, which has progressed from being a traditional smithy to a sizeable concern

John Brennan of Kilkenny, framed in one of his gates.

with a catalogue of many attractive designs made from heavy good-quality material. To compete commercially there has been some mechanisation for bending metal into shape and also the introduction of electric welding; the finished articles are galvanised to preserve them and they are then spray painted. By adopting these methods the firm has been successful and established a reputation. Others, like John Brennan of Kilkenny, now aged seventy-three, have remained traditional, and his iron gates are solid and built to last. It is noticeable that throughout the country nearly all the gates to fields are made of iron, the work of the local blacksmith. They are of simple construction, made of thin bars of iron with strengthening pieces which are usually pleasantly curved, and all riveted together. They are usually hung from a stone pillar, with an eye at the top, while at the bottom a projecting vertical rod of iron pivots on a stone set in the ground.

Farriery

A farrier is a person who shoes horses. Most older blacksmiths used to do this, as part of their routine work at the smithy, though the picture has changed dramatically with the advent of the motor car, and today farriers spend a large part of their time travelling to horses all over the country. There are about 11,000 registered mares in Ireland, and the total horse population must be several times this figure. To look after these there are one hundred qualified full-time farriers and an additional two to three hundred blacksmiths. Horses that hunt, race or are used on roads need re-shoeing every three or four weeks; racehorses are also fitted with lightweight racing plates each time they race. The outside horn of a horse's hoof grows at the rate of about half an inch a month, and as the hoof grows outwards an old shoe will begin to pinch.

To be fully employed, a farrier needs about two hundred horses under his care, and it takes about an hour to shoe each one. A small

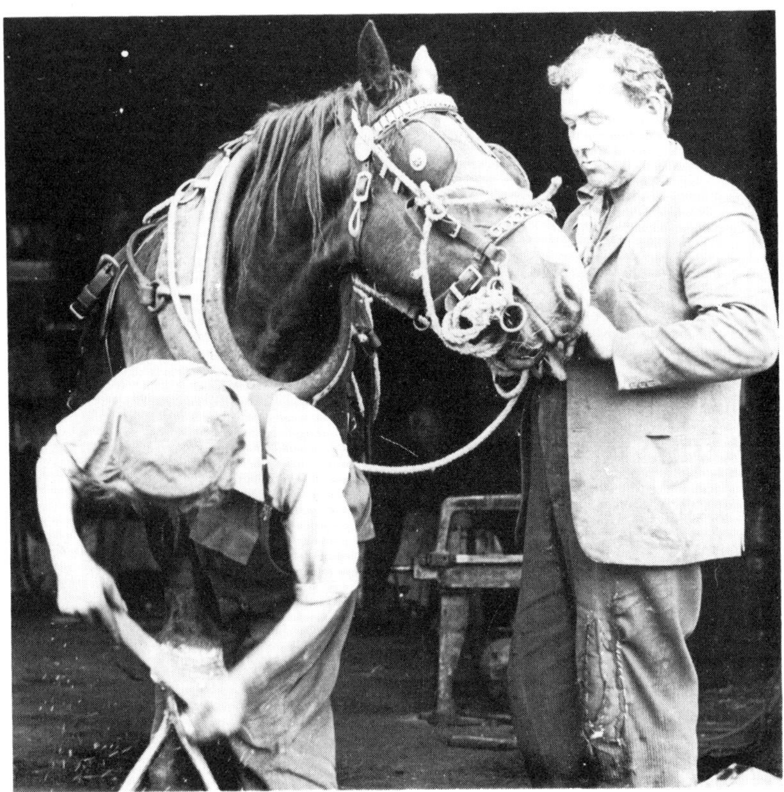

percentage of the horses are either brought to the smithy, if it is within easy reach, or else the animal is brought in a trailer. When this happens the shoe can be fitted 'hot', i.e. the shoe is bedded into the horn of the hoof while still hot; this burns a little of the horn in the process, giving off a cloud of blue smoke that neither worries nor hurts the horse. After fitting, the shoe is cooled in water before being nailed on. Old shoes are removed and kept as a pattern from which to make new ones. Many farriers now buy ready-made shoes from a factory in order to save time and these

Shoeing a jaunting car pony at Killarney, Co. Kerry.

have to be altered to the shape of each particular horse. The alternative is to make the shoes from steel bars and this involves cutting a strip to the right length, bending it to shape, fullering a groove for fitting the nails, and finally punching the nail holes. Farriery is hard work, as all shoeing is done in a very uncomfortable position while holding the horse's hoof between the legs. The farrier wears a thick leather apron as protection, necessary because a horse might move and if the nail has just been inserted it can cause a nasty gash. A travelling farrier nearly always shoes 'cold': a shoe can have minor alterations done to it without heating, so that the fit is satisfactory; moreover, highly-strung thoroughbreds are generally too nervous to have hot shoes put on.

Many sons follow their father's footsteps in the trade. Typical is Tom Mellerick of Dangan, Co. Cork, a fifth generation farrier. He still makes all his own shoes and is busiest between September and April, during the hunting and point-to-point seasons. New farriers must now be qualified and it is a craft that is becoming increasingly scientific and specialised, at a time when racehorses are worth vast sums of money.

Spade-making

The making of spades by hand is a craft that still lingers on, though it appears that the only remaining practitioners are brothers Robert and Jack Patterson of Templepatrick, Co. Antrim, whose family have been making them for almost two hundred years. Formerly, firms turning them out in small numbers enabled the regional differences in design to persist, and these were preferred to factory-made products. The Pattersons make twelve different varieties of spades. These include turf slanes, shovels, draining and Fermanagh spades. The latter is designed primarily for turning over heavy sods and is really more of a hand plough than a digging tool. For digging, long-handled shovels are generally used.

The spades are made out of mild steel, bought in long bars, and small blocks are cut appropriate to the type of spade being manufactured; for example, for a Fermanagh spade a piece of 4 inches by 3 inches, and weighing about 3 pounds is needed. All operations are done with the metal heated to a red glow. The first machine cuts the shoulders from the block and makes an indentation that will eventually become the socket hole. The metal is then re-heated, put under a heavy trip hammer and moved along about an inch after every blow. The hammer itself is a museum piece one hundred years old and is operated by a water turbine, which replaced a waterwheel some years ago. The lump of metal slowly becomes elongated and is re-heated from time to time, being held in the fire with a pair of tongs. The hammering slowly draws out the blade of the spade and then the straps on either side of the socket hole are similarly extended by hammering, having had dust sprinkled between them to prevent the hammer blows welding them together. The hammering and heating continues until the spade is the required size, a low relief herring-bone pattern being left on the face of the blade by the hammer. The blade is then trimmed around the edges in a hand-shearing machine, and the socket hole is opened up with a mandrel. It is then heated again and shaped in a press to give it the right curvature, a different mould being used for each type of spade. The ash handle is placed in the socket and secured by rivets, and the straps rounded to the handle under pressure. Footplates are then electrically welded to the shoulders and the finished spade is then given a coat of paint or varnish. The Patterson brothers turn out about one hundred spades a week, and each costs about the same as a factory-produced spade, with the advantage that the latter can be made to the specific size required.

6
WOOL WORKERS

Spinning and Dyeing

The hand-spinning of wool for commercial purposes is dying out as it cannot compete with the speed and uniform thickness of that produced by machine. On the other hand, an increasing amount is being done by enthusiasts who like to buy fleeces and then sort, card, spin and dye the wool. The finished yarn can then be either knitted or woven. An important cottage industry, spinning was done by women and children. There are a large number of wheels in the older cottages, many of them antique heirlooms, and most of the older people know how to spin, having learnt the art in their youth. Although there is once more a demand for hand-spun wool from craft shops, which sell it in the form of finished knitted garments, adequate supplies are no longer available, as it is a poorly-paid form of employment.

There are a number of different kinds of spinning wheel. In Kerry they are mostly of the hand-operated kind, in which the right hand is used for turning the wheel and the left for feeding the wool. The spindle is held in position by strands of twisted straw.

Elsewhere there are treadle types such as the Donegal and Northern Irish, which differ in detail and can be used for spinning flax as well as wool. The wool also varies in character, depending on the breed of sheep and the part of the body it comes from, so it must be carefully sorted. In most weaving areas the blackface sheep predominates, and produces a hard wool containing a proportion of hair which will not dye. Dyes that were used came from local sources such as lichens, onion skins, heath, water lily, etc., and a combination of some of these produced the well known

60

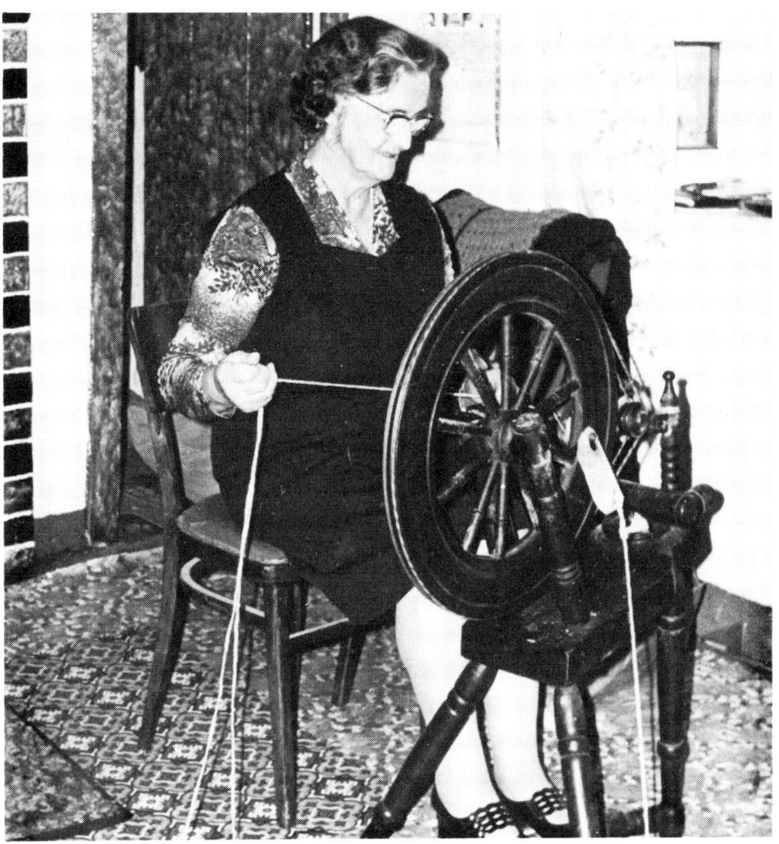

'salt and pepper' look associated with Donegal tweed.

Until about thirty years ago William McNelis of Ardara dyed the wool straight from the sheep's back. He has been weaving for fifty years, is a third generation weaver, and his three sons have followed him into the craft. He dyes the wool in a cauldron of water: a layer of wool is followed by a layer of dye and so on until the cauldron is full. This is boiled for $^3/_4$ hour, then washed and dried. Oil is then added and the wool carded by combing with hand

*Gerald McNelis, a fourth
generation weaver at work in
Ardara, Co. Donegal.*

carders to get the fibres running parallel, then it is spun and finally woven.

Hand-weaving

Donegal is the stronghold of hand weaving, which has always been an important cottage industry. It has survived in the area because of a lack of other profitable employment, and it fitted in with the work of a smallholding which in itself did not provide a living. Marketing of the finished cloth always presented the weaver with problems, but a successful organisation has been built up by the firm of Magees in Donegal. In the past individual weavers made cloth of differing quality, weight and design so there was little uniformity in the finished product. Now materials and patterns, with exact instructions, are sent out to weavers within a thirty mile radius of Donegal and the finished cloth is later collected. Magees are one of the world's biggest sellers of handwoven cloth with between seventy and eighty weavers who are all men—the work is physically demanding—and about two-thirds of production is exported. Most of the yarn is bought from other mills and warped on to a beam, a long wooden roller, on which the threads are woven in an exact sequence in order to produce the desired pattern. A double width beam can have around 1200 separate threads with a length of seventy yards which is normal for each finished bolt of cloth.

The weaver places the beam on his loom and then passes every thread through the heddles, small wire eyes attached to the reed. Setting up a loom takes about five hours for a double width cloth and it is slow, exacting work. Warp thread is wound into three or four shuttles on the loom, each having a different colour of thread, depending on the pattern. When operating the loom the weaver flicks the shuttle to and fro using a string in his right hand. With his left hand he raises and lowers the box containing the shuttles; this alters the colours of the warp thread. The left hand also operates the sley which beats up the last woven warp thread. At the same time the feet are used to work the reeds, which lift the heddles to produce the required pattern. There may be up to six reeds to be operated if the pattern is complicated.

The simplest weave is 'tabby' in which each thread passes over one and under one; it can be done using one reed and one shuttle, usually with a white warp and a flecked weft. Twill and herringbone are a little more complicated, as are the checks.

The weaver has to concentrate all the time, keeping a sharp eye to see that there are no broken threads. The shuttle thread also needs periodic replenishing. Of the looms that supply Magees about one third weave single-width cloth of thirty inches, a third weave double width of about seventy inches, while the remainder are 'Hattersley' looms which are powered by foot and are semi-automatic. The amount of cloth a weaver can produce depends on the thickness of the thread, the complexity of the pattern, the width of the cloth, and the speed with which the weaver works. Every piece bears his signature declaring it to be hand woven, using pure new wool.

After the cloth is woven it is brought to the factory for finishing. First it is inspected for flaws, knots and breakages and the defects are invisibly mended. It is then washed, shrunk and pressed. The quality of the water is important, rainwater being best. Mills are always situated where there is an ample supply of water, originally used for driving the machinery, and also required for washing and finishing.

In the north of Donegal hand-weaving almost died out a few years ago, but has been revived by the firm of McNutt, of Downings. Scot McNutt trained in textiles and on his return to the firm suggested that instead of tweed cloth, hard to sell during the recession of the early 1970s, the firm should concentrate on weaving top quality furnishing materials with attractive designs

Hand looms for making furniture materials, at McNutts of Downings, Co. Donegal.

and a slightly rough finish. The enterprise has been successful and the cloth is now sold to an increasing number of furniture manufacturers throughout the world.

Another successful enterprise, rescued at the last moment, is Avoca Handweaving in Avoca, Co. Wicklow. Until twenty-five years ago each operation was done on the premises, and comprised dyeing, spinning and weaving. It then ran down and, in 1974, was on the point of closure when a solicitor, Donald Pratt, took it over, revived it, and today it is a thriving concern. There are twelve handloom weavers, ten wooden and two Hattersley looms. The aim is to provide attractive quality designs, a policy that has proved so successful that the finished articles are exported to all parts of the world, and include cloth, bedspreads, travel rugs, jackets and hoods.

One comparatively new and expanding business is the 'Weavers Shed' in Dublin, inspired by Noreen Kennedy. After learning to weave at art college and practical experience in a mill in Galashiels, on the Scottish Borders, she set up as a weaver in Duke Street, Dublin. Orders increased and the opportunity came nine years ago to buy a disused mill. Helped by her father, machinery was installed and there has since been a steady expansion: the workforce has now increased to twenty-five including four handloom weavers. Their products include kaftans, tabards, skirts, rugs, and tweeds.

'Irish Tapestries' of Drogheda, Co. Louth, produce an attractive range of bedspreads and pillow covers, employing outworkers who hand-knot the bedspreads and finish off the fringes. They export ninety-five per cent of their output to Harrods and exclusive shops in Italy, and cushions to Japan. In common with other successful enterprises a major factor is the skill of the designers. Patterns are becoming much more enterprising, combining more colours and different textured materials to cope with the increasing demands of fashion. Trade is becoming more international and businesses must export in order to survive, so there must be a steady flow of new designs with a premium on hand-work and craftsmanship.

Tweed Hats

Galway has established a reputation for tweed hats and now exports them all over the world. The long-established firm of

Making tweed hats at Millars in Clifden, Co. Galway.

Millars of Clifden, Co. Galway, makes the best-selling tweed hat in the world, with one American shop alone taking no less than one thousand a week. The hats are made of coarse durable wool, mostly from Scottish blackface sheep, and Millars are unusual in that they do each process themselves. Everything was hand-spun until about twenty years ago, although their rugs are still hand-woven. Their success lies in the combination of attractive designs and colours so that the customer can have either a traditional hat or one that is more fashionable. A great deal of the work is still done by hand, such as the cutting, stitching, trimming and ironing, so that

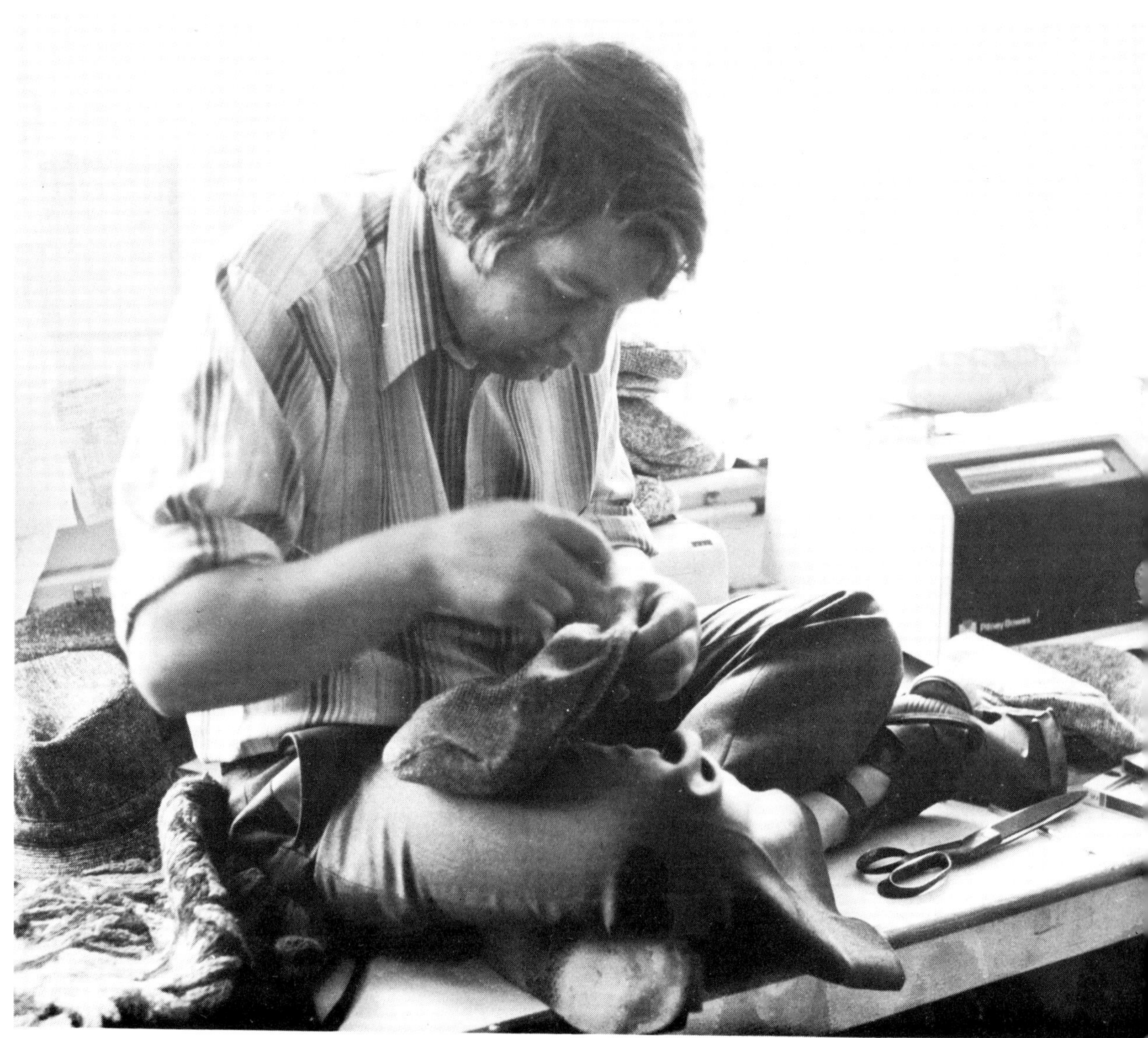

craftmanship still plays a major part in the finished article.

Another successful hatmaker in Clifden is David Hanna, who is now assisted by his four sons. A man of many parts, having been a boxer, swimmer, athlete and tailor, he began by making and designing hats ten years ago, sitting on a bench crossed-legged, doing the hand-stitching. He only uses Irish woven cloth and designs all the hats himself, using bright colours and bold designs of a kind now popular in men's fashions. His expanding business also sends its wares all over the world, and particularly to America.

Sprigging and Crochet

The stronghold of sprigging is in the Mount Charles area of Co. Donegal. Sprigging consists of the hand-embroidering of linen, and is slow and exacting work which is now only practised by an ever-decreasing number of older women. Similar work of an excellent quality can be produced by sophisticated modern sewing machines, but even these require highly-skilled operators. The most commonly produced articles include table mats and cloths made of linen stitched with cotton embroidery thread.

Patterns are ironed on to cloth and give a blue outline to guide the worker. A typical article is a banqueting table-cloth measuring perhaps twelve by six feet. When finished it will sell for about IR£80 if machine-embroidered and only IR£100 if hand-produced, the difference in cost being comparatively small in view of the time taken to stitch by hand. As there is sales resistance above this price it is impossible to pay the handworker well, as it would price the article out of the market, and this is a case where the homeworker might be better off drawing unemployment payments.

A typical cottage worker is Mrs Minnie Wilson, who makes about one table-cloth a month. She stretches the pattern tight in a small circular embroidery frame and, with her nimble fingers, works with

Stitching a Hanna hat at Clifden, Co. Galway.

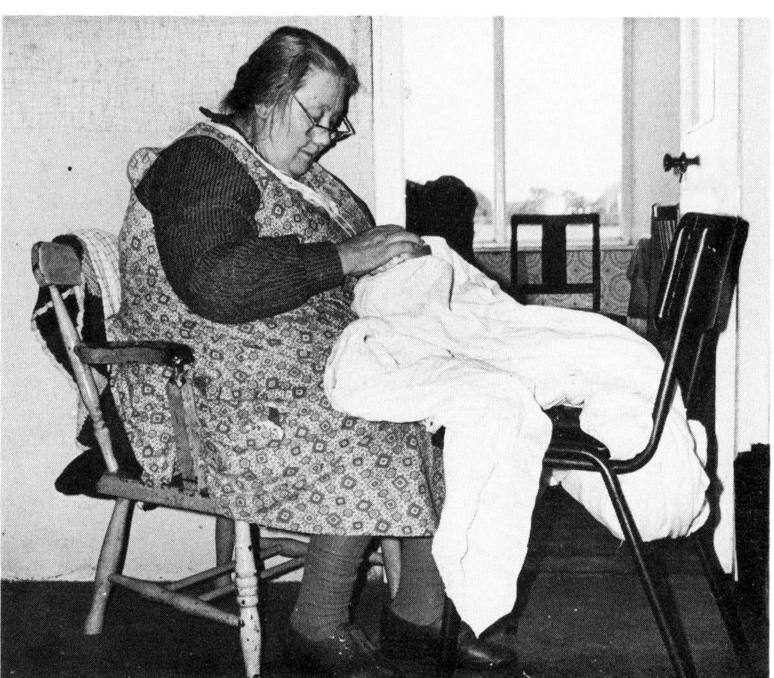

great speed and accuracy. On completion the table-cloth is sent for finishing; this can involve the addition of a lace edging or perhaps a hand rolled edge.

Aran Sweaters

Aran sweaters are famous throughout the world for their warmth and attractive appearance. As their name implies they originally came from the Aran Islands off the Connemara coast, were made for fishermen from unwashed and thick ply yarn for winter wear and were very warm. Sometimes they were dyed green with cabbage leaves. Originally the spinning was done by women and

An Aran islander with a knitted sweater.

men did the knitting. Now they are knitted all over Ireland and are to be seen on sale throughout the country. Though attempts have been made, they cannot be produced satisfactorily by machine and are all hand-knitted. They take about one week to knit, and sell for about £30 in shops, of which the knitter gets around forty pence an hour. They are knitted with three or four ply wool in white or slightly off-white, and it is almost impossible to obtain one that still retains the natural oil.

There are about ten to twelve different kinds of stitches that can be used in a variety of different permutations. All Aran families used to have their different and individual patterns of sweaters. Some of the stitches in common use are:

1. **Trinity** or **blackberry** stitch, which has a religious significance, and is formed by multiples of three stitches.
2. **Cables,** representing the fisherman's ropes.
3. **Plaited cable,** which indicates the interweaving of family life.
4. **Honeycomb,** representing the hard work and toil in the beehive.
5. **Trellis,** which represents the small fields surrounded by their stone walls.
6. **Zigzag,** symbolises the rugged cliffs and winding paths, and is combined with marriage lines to show the ups and downs of married life.
7. **The ladder of life** symbolises man's desire to reach to eternal life and happiness.
8. **Moss** stitch for wealth and the abundant growth of mossy soil.
9. **Diamond,** the symbol of success and wealth.

Donegal Carpets

There are very few firms in Europe still making hand-woven carpets, but one survivor is Donegal Carpets of Killybegs, Co. Donegal. The industry was founded eighty years ago and at one time there were four small factories but the depression of the 1930s reduced this to one. Since then this solitary survivor has taken on a new lease of life: today there are thirty girl weavers, or tufters, and business is good. Making hand-knotted woollen carpets is slow work and in consequence the finished article is fairly expensive,

Weaving Donegal carpets at Killybegs.

though its long-wearing properties make it a good investment.

Apart from the wearing qualities, the advantages of hand-made carpets are that they can be made to any design, colour and shape, to fit in with an existing decor, and up to forty feet in width without a seam. They are ideal for prestige buildings, and examples are to be found in Buckingham Palace, the White House, the Dorchester Hotel and Lancaster House. Another example is a recently-completed carpet for Arlington Court, in Devon, a property belonging to the National Trust. This carpet was designed as a replacement for an antique carpet, embodies a family crest, and is reproduced in the subtle shades of the original for which wool had to be dyed to the exact shades required, in addition to being moth-proofed. The finished carpet is about eighteen feet in width and took six girls about three months to complete.

To make a carpet the girls sit facing a vertical frame and each knots a section about three feet in width. The design is transferred to a pattern consisting of a large number of small squares on graph paper, and these are pinned on the frame in front of each tufter, who ties the knots according to this pattern. The warp threads are of flax, from Belfast, and are secured to a large wooden beam over-head. As work progresses the finished carpet is wound on to another beam below and behind the frame. Short lengths of wool of the relevant colour are placed at hand between the warp threads and these are taken for knotting as required. Every piece is hand-knotted, about twenty-five to the square inch, and each knot secures two warp threads. After knotting her section a girl beats the work down tight with a small toothed fork, combs out the wool, and trims it to a length with scissors. When a row of knots has been completed right across the carpet by all the girls, two warp threads are passed through the weft and the next row of knots is tied. When the carpet has been fully woven it is wound on to a wide wooden beam, and sheared to give an exact and even thickness to the pile.

7
STRAW, RUSH & WILLOW

Thatching

Thatch used to be the roof of the poor man as the materials were cheap and convenient, and the work comparatively easy, using local methods. It had the disadvantage, however, of lasting only a year or two in most cases. Some purpose-built cottages are also covered with thatch, such as in the town of Adare, and specially built Bord Fáilte holiday homes, as well as cottages at the folk parks of Bunratty, Glencolumbkille, the Ulster Folk Museum, and the buildings in the Craggaunowen restored ring fort complex. In these cases the work has been done by professionals to a high standard and in consequence the thatch will last a good deal longer, having a life-span of between ten and twenty years.

Notable features rarely met elsewhere are the low angle of pitch of the roofs. Nearly all have a slope of forty-five degrees, which is the minimum for allowing the rain to run off. Leggetts or beaters are rarely used to tighten up the thatch; in consequence it is very loosely laid and hence does not have a long life. Most roofs have a layer of turf sods, scraws or scrolls laid on the rafters, and these are

tied in place with twine, straw rope or hung with wooden pegs. The
sods are about two inches thick, and are laid like slates, grass side
downwards. The thatch covering goes over these. The thatch can
be of reed, wheat, oat, barley or rye straw, marram grass or sedge. In
the past potato haulms, heather and flax were also occasionally
used. Rye straw is much favoured and often small plots of it are
specially grown for thatching, notably in the Aran Islands where all
the remaining thatch is of this material. Barley straw is used least of

Thatching with rye straw in Donegal.

all, while marram grass is pulled by its roots which are laid uppermost when laying the thatch; in the past rye was similarly pulled.

Most thatching consists of laying the materials on the roof to a thickness of about four inches on a very still day, so that it will not blow about, and immediately covering it with chicken wire or old fish netting, or by roping it down. Using this method a new layer can be put on in one or two days but this has the disadvantage of lasting for only one or two years. In some districts the custom is to renovate one side of the roof each year so the complete roof is renewed every two. Another practice is to dip the sheaves in a solution of 'blue steel' to preserve it. This is a fungicide that used to be sprayed on potatoes before more modern chemicals became available, and it extends the life of the straw.

When reed is used it is secured by wooden scallops, which are cut from sallies. A scallop is laid horizontally across the reed and held in position by further scallops which are bent into the shape of a hairpin and pushed into the reed. As the thatchter works upwards the scallops are covered until the ridge is reached. The treatment of the ridge varies with the type of thatch. Reed does not bend so it is normally butted at the top and sometimes a covering is placed over this of some other straw that will bend, and this is held down by scallops. Most other roofs are rounded on top.

A thatcher in the Lough Derg area, using sedge, butts it by looping it over a rod of willow and pegging it down. In most cases the bottom row of thatching material is tied to the rafters by twine. Most thatchers prefer to work in lanes, starting at the bottom and working up the roof, doing a strip at a time. This means that the ladder, an essential piece of equipment for all thatchers, does not have to be moved so often. A precaution taken by most careful thatchers is to tie the bottom of the ladder so that it will not slip. In windy areas, particularly along the west coast, most houses have eyebolts built into the masonry just below the roof line so that

holding-down ropes can be secured. The roping is sometimes reinforced by hanging stones or horizontal metal bars to hold down the thatch against the force of the gales. One problem is that the thatch has very little overhang at the eaves, and much of the rainwater runs down the walls instead of being thrown clear.

Very many cottages with thatched roofs are of a great age, rather small and lacking modern facilities, so that with increasing prosperity they are beginning to be replaced by modern and less attractive bungalows. Thatching is on the decline and with it will go

A typical thatched cottage with the thatching straw held down by ropes weighted with stones.

the little whitewashed thatched-roof cottages that are such an attractive feature of the Irish countryside.

Rushwork

Articles made of rushes can be seen in most craft shops. Most of this work comes from the Slieve Bawn Co-operative Handicraft Market Ltd, of Strokestown, Co. Roscommon. Under the guiding hand of Patsy Duignan the co-operative has prospered and high standards of craftsmanship and design have been set over the twenty years of its existence. It embodies all types of craft, but chiefly rushwork, and now has about two hundred women at work in their homes. The type of rush used is *scirpus lacrustus*, which grows profusely around the edge of rivers and ponds. The rushes grow to a height of between five and seven feet and the best are grown in running water, which makes them slightly softer than those from lakes. They are cut with a sickle or hook and then floated ashore. After cutting they are put on a trailer to avoid bending, as any damage or bruising renders the rushes useless. They have to be harvested around the longest day of the year because if left much longer they become brittle. They are then dried with a good circulation of air, during which they develop a powdery mould which falls off like dust. When properly dry the colour varies from green to brown, and they keep indefinitely if properly cured. The rushes are then placed in a bath of water for a short time, sometimes with the addition of detergent to clean them; they are then removed, wrapped in a towel and flattened.

An article like a basket is made on a 'former' of wood and hardboard in the shape of the finished piece. The rushes are interwoven over the former using a variety of weaves such as check, twill and pairing, which gives the completed article style and character. It takes about an hour for a skilled worker to make a small basket, which has to be carefully dried; it is then usually

A rush basket being made for the
Slieve Bawn Co-operative at
Strokestown, Co. Roscommon.

given a coat of varnish which helps to preserve it and gives an attractive finish. The work is easy on the hands as the moist rushes are soft and pliable, and most of it is done by women.

Besides baskets, rushes are a suitable material for table mats and the making of St Brigid's crosses. For St Brigid's day (1 February), crosses used to be made for every room in the house by interweaving rushes, though they could also be made of straw, hay or any such material. The crosses ensure the saint's blessing and protection on the household, animals and crops for the ensuing year. In spite of the increased production the demand cannot be met, half the output being exported. The materials cost little or nothing, although time, labour and care in drying are required to produce satisfactory material.

Basket-making

The craft of basket-making is widespread and mostly done by individuals to meet a local demand; there is very little surplus for sales in the craft shops, which are clamouring for them. There are a few full-time professional basket-makers such as the Shanahan brothers of Carrick-on-Suir, Co. Tipperary, who used to be the largest in the business employing a number of craftsmen, reduced now to the two brothers who no longer work full-time. The Quinlan brothers of Tallow, Co. Waterford, turn out a fair number, combining this skill with their work as water-bailiffs. Thomas Quinlan says that eighteen years ago you could not give baskets away, and this drastically reduced the numbers making them. Now the market cannot be satisfied and craft shops have difficulty getting supplies; the few remaining makers prefer to sell direct to customers as it is more profitable than selling to retailers. John Delaney of Limerick, now aged seventy-four, has been making baskets all his life in a long established business, while a newcomer to the craft is Joe Hogan of Lough Nafooey, Co. Galway,

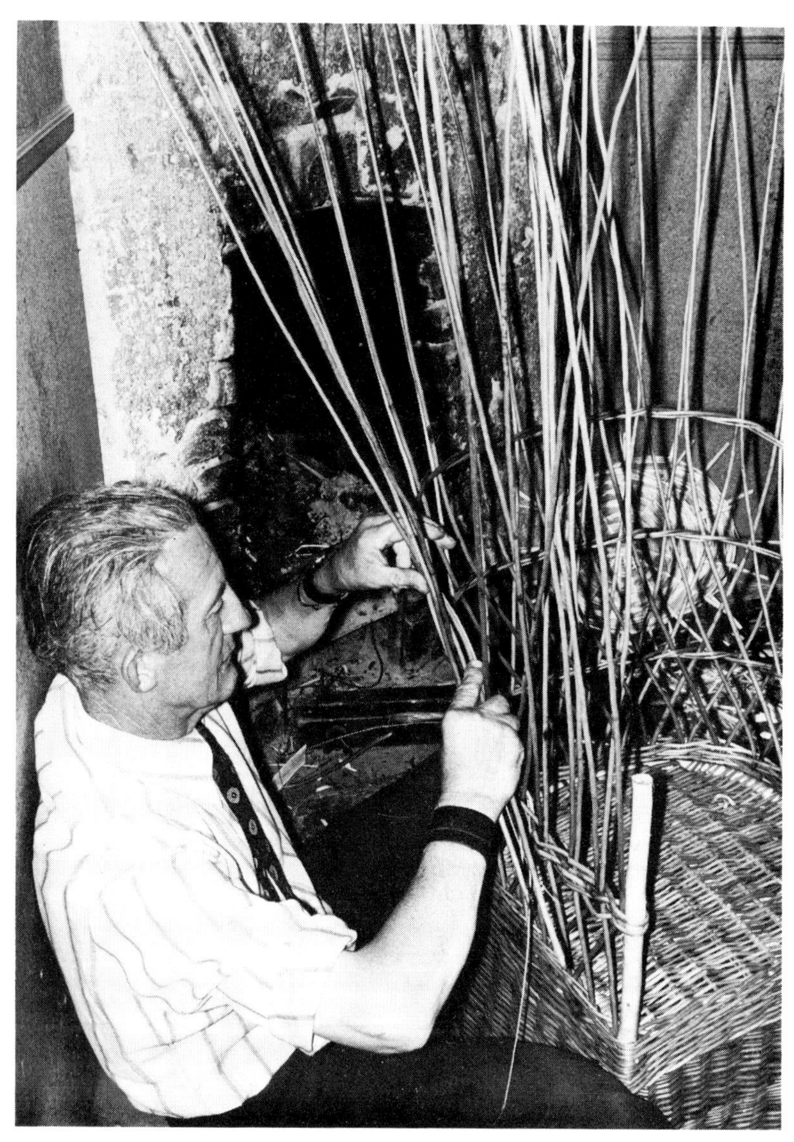

Thomas Quinlan of Tallow, Co. Waterford, weaving a garden chair out of willow rods.

who, having obtained an academic degree, has since retired to the country to carry out full-time basket work.

Baskets are made from the wood of willow, of which there are a bewildering number of species. Most widely used are 'sallies', from willows that can be seen growing by the roadside. Usually the rods are cut off at about head height, and are worked while still fresh

John Delaney making a wicker chair in Limerick.

and pliable. The other type is referred to as 'osiers', and most of these are imported from England or Holland. Osier rods are cut off at ground level every year and form stools which grow to a height of around seven feet during the summer.

Thomas Quinlan thinks he is one of the very few growers of this type of willow in Ireland as the place where he works as a water-bailiff has the right conditions and he is able to cut his willow every year; failure to do so renders the willow useless as it grows large and pithy. He grows his willow from a short stump about two feet high, cutting the rods in January and leaving them standing in water till the spring, when they can be peeled to give a pleasant, white appearance. The other method is to boil the rods before peeling and the tannin from the bark stains these an attractive brown colour. Willows are similarly grown around Roscommon and Joe Hogan has planted a small acreage of various different varieties, although he will have to wait a few years to see the results. Some of his species are an attractive red colour and others yellow, in addition to the normal type for making white or buff rods.

There are two different ways of making baskets. The conventional method, used in many parts of the world, is for the craftsman to sit on the ground, with a wooden board in front of him, on which he makes the basket. By his side are his tools, few and simple, and his willow rods, which have previously been soaked in water to make them pliable. Starting at the base, the basket is built up using a variety of different weaves such as randing, slewing, fitching, and waling. By these methods baskets can be made for dogs, logs, shopping, picnics or garden chairs, for all of which there is a very strong demand.

The alternative method of making baskets, usually called creels, is to use long sallies which are pushed into the ground to a depth of about six inches in the shape of the basket. This will form the top of the basket, which is built upside-down, and at the finish will have the rods that were in the ground protruding from the basket top.

Basket-making in the Aran Islands.

Usually the middle part of the basket is left with a good deal of openwork which keeps it light and speeds the work. This is quite satisfactory for turf and long baskets but for other produce, such as potatoes, the gaps must be kept small. The bottom is finished last by twisting and interweaving the sallies across the base. Some peat baskets for fitting over the backs of donkeys are made with flat sides and have hinged lids on the bottom so that the load can be

85

emptied easily. Both lids have to be opened simultaneously or the load will become lopsided. With the introduction of tractors or cars and trailers, however, the donkey population has declined drastically, and with it the demand for this type of basket.

Another common type of basket is the potato lean. This is saucer-shaped, about a foot in diameter, and is used for straining water from potatoes that have been boiled in their jackets. To make one a willow is first bent to form a circle and the ends secured. Then two rods are fixed to the circle to form the belly of the lean; this enables it to lie flat and not topple over. A few more ribs are added and are all held in place by cross-weaving small pliable rods round the rim and acrosss the belly. Attractive effects can be obtained by using rods of different coloured willow, some red, some brown and others yellow.

One difficulty that all craftsmen encounter is getting paid, and a reminder of this can be seen in Tom Quinlan's workshop. It runs:

> *Our work is good,*
> *Our terms are just,*
> *Forgive us for we cannot trust;*
> *We have trusted many to our sorrow,*
> *Please pay today and owe tomorrow.*

8
COOPERS & WHEELWRIGHTS

Coopers

A cooper is a craftsman who makes wooden casks, more usually called barrels. In practice all existing coopers are employed making barrels for whiskey. Since whiskey has to be matured in wooden barrels, oak being the most suitable wood, it looks as if there is a good future for this craft. Coopering requires skill that can only be acquired over a number of years, the work depending on accuracy and fine judgement of the eye that can only be gained by experience. There are around twenty coopers at the Middleton distillery complex in Co. Cork, a similar number at Power's in Dublin and nine at the Old Bushmills distillery in Co. Antrim.

A curious fact is that all the wood is second-hand oak from North America. Bourbon whiskey by law has to be put in new barrels and when empty these are shaken down by dismantling, and imported by Irish distillers. The whiskey industry is expanding, so there is a steady demand for more barrels, and repair work is also needed on existing barrels which have been emptied after the whiskey has matured and then re-used. By law whiskey must be matured in the

wood for a minimum of three years and it is usually left a good deal
longer. Old sherry and port butts are also good for maturing but
they are becoming harder to obtain. With careful handling barrels

can be used indefinitely, and it is quite usual to find fifty-year-old barrels in use.

American bourbon barreis have a capacity of about 40 gallons and are charred on the inside as a means of sterilisation. As the barrels are hand-made their capacity is never exact, the actual capacity being inscribed on the lid. To assemble them reqires great skill, particularly during the first stage of 'raising'. The cooper takes a single metal trussing hoop and sets a bundle of staves one by one around the hoop. This operation demands great delicacy of touch or all the staves will collapse. Having successfully placed the top hoop in position, a larger hoop is placed over the barrel and forced down, locking the staves together. The barrel can then be reversed and hoops placed around the other end.

Next comes the fitting of the lids. A groove is cut on the inside of the barrel, near the top, using a circular plane called a cross which is specially made for the task. The hoops are eased to enable the staves to be opened sufficiently for the lid to be dropped into place. A rush is then placed round the groove and this gives the lid a watertight fit. The hoops are driven down hard over the staves using a tool called a driver, which is belted down with a heavy hammer, and such is the accuracy with which the staves are made that the finished barrel will be watertight. Finally, a circular hole is drilled in the centre of the bulge for filling, which is sealed with a wooden bung.

Traditionally, whiskey is stored in the barrels in a damp cellar and the humidity and temperature play an important part in the subtlety and delicacy of the final flavour. As the wood is slightly porous, there is a small loss over the maturing years, and each is occasionally topped up. It staits as a colourless liquid, and obtains some of its golden colour from the barrel and some from the addition of caramel at a later stage.

Coopering used to be a far more extensive craft. Stephen Daly of Ennis, Co. Clare, now over seventy, is a third generation cooper.

Though he can turn his hand to all aspects of the craft, he now mostly makes ornamental tubs on a part-time basis. Among the articles made earlier in his career were wooden firkins, in which butter was sold in the Ennis market up to 1948. These had six sally hoops at each end, weighed 12 lbs and held 70 lbs of butter. In his workshop hangs the cooper's banner with the inscription, 'Brothers of the Oak'. His work has always been in oak, usually American, though the best used to come from Memel in the Baltic. There also used to be a steady demand for churns, cream tubs and end-over-end churns for making butter. With the advent of centralised dairies and creameries, however, this work ceased. A further use for his barrels was bacon salting, still practised in some of the remoter districts.

Wheelwrights and Coachbuilders

One business that has not only survived, but flourished, is the coachbuilding works of Colin Breen at Enniscorthy, Co. Waterford. His workshop is like a transport museum of carriages, horse-traps and coaches, with vehicles in all stages of construction and repair. The firm was founded by his grandfather in 1883 and there are now a dozen employees, making it one of the largest of its type in the world.

A coachbuilder has to be five tradesmen: wheelwright, body-builder, coach smith, coach painter and upholsterer. The firm carries out repairs and restores old carriages, as well as making new ones from any of a hundred designs of different horse-drawn vehicles for which, surprisingly, there is still a small but steady demand. In many parts of the country horse-drawn carts are used for transporting milk to dairies and produce to markets, and of course there are jaunting cars, particularly in the Killarney area, and an increasing number of horse-drawn holiday caravans. The wheels of the latter are invariably pneumatic car wheels but the

90

jaunting cars have craftsman-made wheels. Most also have wooden shafts so there is plenty of work in certain areas for the few remaining craftsmen.

Seasoned wood from particular trees is a prime essential for all work connected with wheelwrights. The hubs or stocks are of elm, though they can also be made of metal, the spokes of heart of oak, felloes that form the rim of a wheel can also be of oak, beech or ash, and shafts of ash, while the frames for coachwork are also mostly of ash. All this wood is best seasoned over a number of years after it has been carefully selected for quality. A wheelwright is one of the few craftsmen who likes to use curved pieces of wood so that he can avoid cutting across the grain whenever possible, thus making his work stronger.

About half of Colin Breen's work is new, and much of it is exported. Many of the metal fittings have been rescued from derelict vehicles, although many new pieces also have to be made. Tyres are also shrunk on to wheels, a job requiring a blacksmith and at least two assistants. Vehicles for the show ring have to be immaculate, calling for workmanship of the highest quality. They are finished off with special coach enamel from Harrisons of Dublin, several coats being needed as well as much rubbing down before the final finishing coat is applied.

There are a number of other men of sixty years and upwards who were wheelwrights when younger and who can still cope with some of the work with occasional help from a blacksmith. Michael Lines of Ennis, Co. Clare, is a fourth generation wheelwright who made his last wheel twelve years ago. He has since turned his hand to such objects as trailers, barrows and garden seats. Nowadays, a good carpenter or joiner can cope with much of the wheelwright's work, with the exception of wheel repairs which must be carried out by an expert using seasoned wood.

9
SPORTS WARE

Fishing Rods

Irish lakes and rivers are renowned for their fishing and there is consequently a big demand for rods. Nowadays most are of glass fibre and consequently are imported together with a number of split cane rods. However, others are still made of greenheart, which used to be the most sought after type until the virtual disappearance of the wood from the market. It is greenish in colour, very heavy and strong, and comes from South America. Another of its properties, apart from its durability, is that it is relatively undamaged by water. Until about fifty years ago it was used extensively by the water authorities for wooden jetty piles, locks and the balancing poles for their gates. Some of this wood occasionally comes on the market and finds its way to Tommy Flynn of Loch Arrow, Co. Sligo, who now makes a few for his friends, chiefly for pleasure rather than as a full-time occupation. He makes them in two sections for trout and three for salmon; these are rods for the conoisseur and are much treasured by the favoured few who are fortunate to obtain one.

Tommy Flynn of Lough Arrow,
Co. Sligo, with two of his
greenheart fishing rods.

Another type of hand-made rod, indeed the predominant type before the advent of glass fibre, is the split cane. Making them is rather slow and labourious but well worthwhile in the long run. They are made with a number of carefully and accurately worked pieces of split cane, usually six, that are glued together to form the rod which is very strong and has just the right amount of whip. About a dozen of them are made each year by Michael Rogan, the well-known fly dresser of Ballyshannon, Co. Donegal. Each one is signed and, as well as being a highly desirable piece of equipment, is also a good investment which will appreciate in value.

Fishing Flies

The supreme maker of fishing flies is Michael Rogan, whose works are in Ballyshannon. His firm's reputation has been built up over many years since its founding in 1830; a silver medal and diploma were awarded at the London International Exhibition of 1883. Michael Rogan has been fly dressing for over forty years, during which he has gained international fame in fishing circles. The following ode to his prowess comes from Wales:

> *The fly was by Rogan of famed Ballyshannon,*
> *The best man who ever dressed hook for salmon,*
> *All his flies are superb, I assure you tis true,*
> *There is nothing on Conway like his silver and blue.*

His wife is an expert in tying flies, and young, local girls are also trained to make them when they leave school. A remarkable feature of the flies is the fact that they are made with the hands alone, with no vice to hold the hook. Michael Rogan considers that this gives a more delicate and sensitive tension to the silk with which the fly is tied.

Hurling Sticks

The popularity of hurling ensures a large and steady demand for sticks, the best of which are hand-made from ash. One well-known maker is Frank Randall of Killurin, Co. Wexford, the third generation in the business. His best sticks are made from ash trees thirty years old, and his search for these takes him all over the country.

The sticks are made of wood from the base of the tree, where it spreads out from the trunk towards the roots. The grain follows the

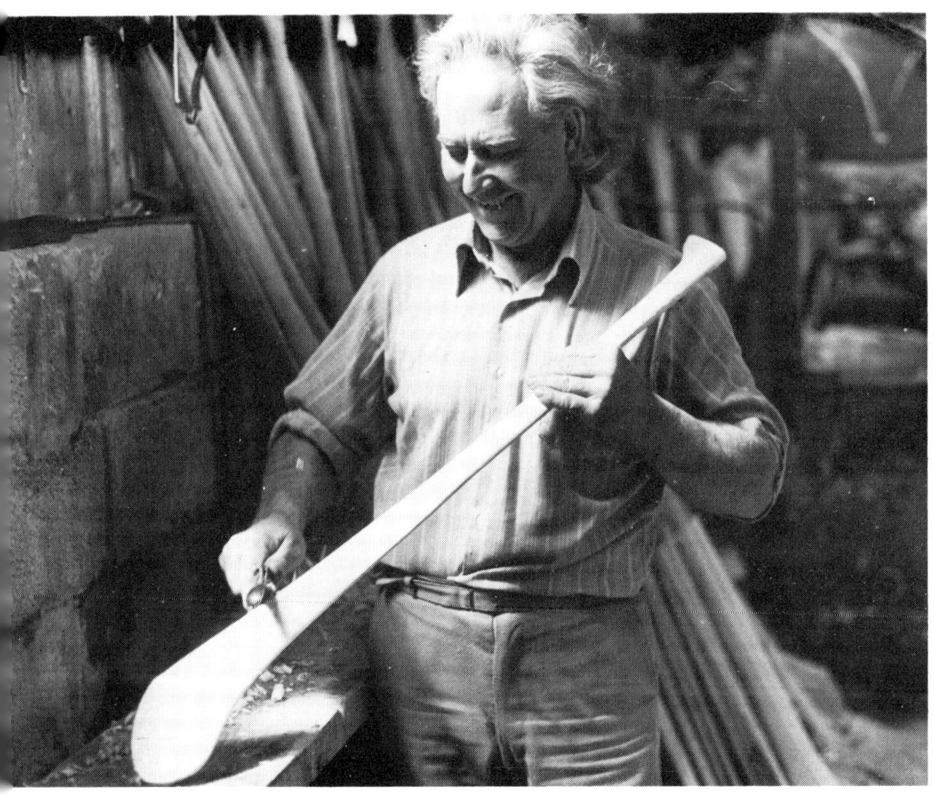

Frank Randall of Killurin, Co. Wexford, putting the finishing touch to a hurling stick.

natural curve of the completed stick, is strong and may be slightly knotted. Should the grain follow the curve exactly, giving a pleasant appearance, the stick will tend to split more easily. The wood is sawn into planks and seasoned by heat, and each butt can provide wood for between three and ten sticks depending on its quality. A curious feature is the fact that the dimensions are not laid down, but in practice the size has become more or less standardised, with the goalkeeper having a slightly larger one. The sticks are first roughly cut to pattern and then machine-shaped into their final dimensions. They then have to be finished off by hand using a spokeshave, followed by sandpapering to give a smooth finish. Finally the maker's name is stamped on and the stick is then ready for use.

Hurling Balls

There is a strong demand for hurling balls, each of which has to be made individually with a certain amount of hand craftsmanship.

Hand-stitching hurling balls at O'Neill's of Dublin.

They are turned out in some quantity by O'Neill's of Dublin, who
employ half a dozen people, each turning out about twenty a day,

*Stitching footballs at O'Neill's, in
Dublin.*

98

or over one hundred a week, although the demand is so strong that it is difficult to keep up with it.

The centre of the ball is made out of a circle of cork about two inches in diameter. Around this polyester thread is wound as tightly as possible. The ball is then dipped in glue to solidify it and keep it watertight. It is then ready to have the white outer leather covering, which is water resistant, sewn on. The leather is cut to shape in a machine and at the same time holes are punched in it to take the stitching. The cover is made up of two pieces of leather in the shape of a figure eight. The seams are saddle stitched with waxed nylon thread, and finally their edges are blackened.

Footballs

O'Neills of Dublin also make footballs for Gaelic, rugby and association football. All are hand stitched with a saddle stitch and are sewn up inside out until the final stages, being held together with a saddler's clamp. Towards the end of the operation a rubber bladder is placed inside and the partially-stitched ball is turned right-side out; this requires a certain amount of persuasion as only a small gap is left for the operation. The final, closing stitches are completed, and the whole is then pulled up tight and fastened securely.

10 INSTRUMENT MAKERS

Harps

Harps have been part of the Irish heritage for many centuries. One of the oldest preserved musical instruments is the 14th century harp in Trinity College, Dublin, and one also appears on Irish coinage, a stylised version of a 'Brian Boru' harp. There has been a revival of interest in the instrument and they are now being bought as quickly as they can be made, with about three-quarters of production being exported. Probably the biggest producer is Waltons, of Dublin, where craftsman Charles Jordan has been making them for twenty years and now has his two sons to help him. Waltons make both Brian Boru knee harps and, more often, the larger Celtic type, a feature of both kinds being the curved shaft or front pillar which is exclusive to Irish harps.

Many centuries ago harps were carved out of willow and occasionally yew, with the sound chamber hollowed out of a single piece of wood. The wood now used for the shaft and scroll is mahogany; it is carefully selected and then seasoned for between seven and ten years. The sound board is of spruce with a beech

*Charles Jordan making a harp
for Walton's of Dublin.*

backing and the sound chamber is of curved ply. The shaft is dovetailed into the scroll and bolted at the bottom of the sound board.

The frame has to be very strong and rigid as it is subjected to

Colm Maher tuning one of his harps.

enormous stress when the strings are set to their proper tension, the strain exerted being as much as half a ton. There are normally thirty-one strings, though this is sometimes increased to thirty-four, all of which are anchored under the sound board, hence the need for the strong beech backing. Strings are preferably of gut, but can also be of nylon or wire. When glue is used it is of the animal type, which is soluble and enables the harp to be dismantled if it needs repairing. After the application of many undercoats and plenty of rubbing down, the final finish is of lacquer. The sound board might then be decorated in a Celtic design by poker work, which is burnt on and then coloured.

Another maker is Colm Maher of Rathfarnham, Dublin, who has been building harps for eight years and produces about twenty each year. All his harps are made to order and with his growing reputation there is currently a six month waiting time for a new one. He uses seasoned sycamore for the main frame and treats all his instruments against woodworm, the scourge of all harps. He uses resin glues, has thirty-four strings of gut or wire, disliking nylon, and applies eight coats of varnish to a high quality finish.

Fiddles

The fiddle is another very popular instrument, and Joe Handley, from the Strokestown area of Co. Roscommon is one man who makes them as a hobby. Having retired from farming he now devotes more time to producing his fine instruments. The delicately shaped and curved back and front are carefully pared down from a single piece of wood until they are a mere sixteenth of an inch thick; this is done by using planes and files, and calls for great skill and patience. He says that there must be tension in the wood to obtain the best tone and that he achieves this by a secret process of his own. The pieces are glued together and the

instruments are finally stained and varnished to give them a good
quality finish.

Uilleann Pipes

Uilleann pipes are exclusively Irish, having been invented
late in the 18th century. They are a truly remarkable invention,
original and complex, and their designer must have been an
instrument maker of great skill and knowledge. Moreover, it is the

Brian Howard of Kilmacow, Co. Waterford, with a set of his uilleann pipes.

only exclusively Irish musical instrument; the nearest equivalent is the Scottish bagpipe, but uilleann pipes are far more sophisticated. They are played in a sitting position and were never designed to be a marching instrument like the bagpipe.

A wind instrument, the pipes have bellows which are placed under the right arm and are used for pumping air into a bag similar to that of the bagpipe. From the bag emerges the chanter which is played with the fingers working the five keys. Also from the bag emerges the cylindrical stock to which are attached three drones, bass, baritone and tenor, with four, four and five keys respectively; a regulator on each drone is operated by the wrist.

One well-known maker is Alf Kennedy of Cork, who has been producing pipes for forty years, first as a hobby, then full-time when he retired from the Garda. He is now helped by his son, also

106

*Brian Howard of Kilmacow,
tuning a set of uilleann pipes.*

makes bagpipes and is booked up for the next three years.

A comparative newcomer to the craft is Brian Howard, a toolmaker from Yorkshire with a great interest in folk music. He was intrigued by the uilleann pipes and started making them eight years ago. His interest became an addiction and one year later he gave up a lucrative job, moved to Kilmacow, Co. Waterford, and started to make them full-time. With his assistant he now turns out about twelve sets a year, in addition to a number of practice bags and chanters.

He has also introduced several innovations. His bags are of cow, instead of sheep hides, and are lined with rubber. Other fittings are made from seamless brass tubes, African hardwood for the chanters and regulators, maghogany and leather bellows, and Spanish cane for the reeds, of which there are no less than seven: one in the chanter, three in each regulator and three in each drone. Brian Howard has also made a wide range of special tools for each of the individual parts, of which there are several hundred in a completed instrument. His tookmaking experience also enables him to make slight modifications so his instruments are continually being improved.

Bagpipes

There is also a steady demand for the Scottish type of bagpipe. These are made by the firm of A. Warnock, of Cookstown, Co. Tyrone, and business is flourishing. The firm has been in existence for twenty-two years, employs five craftsmen, and its products, as well as being used locally, are exported to all parts of the world. The bags are bought ready-made, but the remainder is made on the premises from African hardwood which is turned to make the three drones and the chanter. Some pipes are made of black nylon instead of hardwood, which is not always easy to obtain, and white nylon is used for some of the fittings, which contrasts well with the black hardwood. A few bagpipes are also made in Cork by Alf Kennedy, the well-known maker of uilleann pipes.

Bodhrans

Bodhrans are small drums (the name probably being a corruption of 'tambourine') which are in widespread general use; they are played with a small wooden stick, called a 'bone', and have various different regional shapes. It is said that the best ones are made from greyhound skins though they are normally of goatskin or sheepskin, not calf, which is unsatisfactory. The demand for bodhrans is not sufficient for it to be a full-time occupation so they are produced as a side-line by a number of craftsmen. Some buy vellum while others cure it themselves, but most are reluctant to divulge their methods. The drums are normally some eighteen inches in depth. The frame has supports in the shape of a cross, and the vellum is moistened, stretched over the frame and nailed into position. Vellum is affected by temperature and humidity and if it goes slack can be moistened and dried in the sun.

11 MISCELLANEOUS CRAFTS

Potters

Potteries were always situated where there was a plentiful supply of clay, and the cups, mugs, plates, crocks, roof tiles and bricks they turned out were both important and essential in the days when communities were more or less self-contained. Cups of china or glass were too expensive for ordinary use until the middle of the last century so the demand for pottery was large, the alternative being wood for plates or, more rarely, pewter. The coming of cheaper china put most of the potteries out of business but there has been a revival of the craft and trained potters are now spread throughout Ireland, chiefly on the tourist routes where there is a ready market for their products. Pottery is one of the few crafts where it is possible to make a living and be self-employed from a comparatively early age.

One rare survivor is the famous Belleek pottery in Co. Fermanagh which has been in existence for well over 100 years and has gained a world-wide reputation. The pottery turns out fine china with a characteristic glaze of iridescent lustre. The older

pieces are now much sought after by collectors, particularly those with marine motifs resembling shells, dolphins and mermaids.

Most of the traditional potteries have disappeared, although one

112

notable exception is the remarkable Carley's Bridge Pottery near Enniscorthy in Co. Wexford. Here is the oldest pottery in Ireland and, more extraordinary still, it has been in the same family since 1659 when the two Carley brothers from Cornwall discovered clay in the area and set up business. The firm now concentrates on making pots for horticultural use and they sell their output with ease. There are two traditional types of potter's wheels, which are power driven, and one of the potters is Paddy Murphy, a fifth generation potter with the firm.

Until three years ago the clay was all dug by hand but this is now done mechanically and left outside to weather, when unwanted chemicals in the clay are leached out by frost and rain. When required the clay is fed into the pugging machine, which minces it and breaks down any hard lumps. After pugging it is wedged by hand; this consists of pounding and folding the clay to get it into a workable condition of a suitable consistency.

To make a pot, a lump of clay is thrown on to the wheel and centred. The pot is then raised by the potter's hands, which are continually lubricated. Potters make their work look disarmingly easy, but it takes years of practice. When making pots of a uniform size the pieces of clay must first be weighed. The sides have to be of a uniform thickness throughout, and the slope or curvature must be similar in all pots. This calls for a high degree of skill and craftsmanship.

Paddy Murphy can make pots using 40 lbs of clay for each one. He makes these with surprising speed, taking between five and ten minutes for a pot, and he can throw about eighty of these a day, their weight alone amounting to about one and a half tons. In practice a potter spends only about a third of his time at the wheel and the remainder preparing the clay and taking finished articles to the drying shed.

Every six weeks there is a full load to place in the kiln, which is of the down draught type, brick-built with a domed top. Fires are placed around the circular kiln and the heat goes upwards towards the dome, eventually finding its way to the exhaust flue in the floor. Each firing requires about three tons of coal; this is becoming increasingly expensive, so the kiln must be filled to capacity. It can take approximately 20,000 pots at a time, though the number depends on the size of each. The pots are fired once and the finished articles are then slightly porous. The fires are kept burning continuously for two and a half days and the kiln is then sealed by filling the openings with brick and clay, and cools for another two days before being opened for unloading. Pots made from a grey-coloured clay come out of the kiln red-brown after firing.

The pots are sold at the works for a modest price but by the time they reach the shops the price increases sharply. They are unsurpassed by the modern plastic type which is cheaper and in some ways more convenient, but many horticulturalists still prefer the traditional fired clay pot which Carley's Bridge Pottery produce with such success.

Candles

Candles used to be made of beeswax or tallow fat in which rushes were soaked, though now nearly all are made of paraffin wax by modern factory methods. However at Bunratty Folk Village the old traditional method of dipping is still used. The solid paraffin wax is first melted in a large vat and a frame holding twenty wicks is then dipped into it. During the quick dipping movement a certain amount of wax adheres to the wicks, and the frame is then hung up for a short time to allow the wax to dry. This process is repeated forty times and on each occasion another film of wax sticks to the original core until it is built up into the size needed for a finished candle. The dipping has to be done quickly or the existing wax will melt. The largest maker of church candles is Boramic Ltd, of Borris,

Making candles at Bunratty Folk Village, Co. Clare.

Co. Carlow. These are made by pouring wax into moulds in which special wicks have been fixed. Sometimes the wax is coloured and some of the candles have transfers affixed such as crosses or other religious symbols.

Briar Pipes

The making of briar pipes calls for a good deal of hand craftmanship. The briar wood comes from the Mediterranean area, from the root of *Erica Arborea*, a type of tree heather. The climate produces roots that grow slowly and uniformly and these are harvested when between eighty and 150 years old. Great skill is required in cutting the blocks of wood to avoid waste and to produce the best effect of the grain. The well-known firm of Kapp and Peterson of Dublin, with works at Sallynoggin, has been in business for over one hundred years. Late in the last century they produced the Peterson's system pipe embodying a characteristic shaped bend that produced a cool and dry smoke. Their reputation has been built up by fine craftsmanship and the use of first class materials, and most of the output is now exported to shops throughout the world. Extra refinements consist of nickel, silver or gold bands joining the briar to the stems, which are of ebonite, vulcanite or occasionally amber. Another type of hand-crafted pipe is the 'Meerschaum', made of stone from Turkey and Somalia, although supplies are limited. It has the advantage of being porous, non-inflammable, and relatively light, and the pipes are hand-carved to give a variety of different finishes in a number of colours.

Snuff

Snuff, which is made out of tobacco leaves, is taken on a small scale but is steadily gaining in popularity, particularly in places where smoking is not allowed, such as in mines, some factories and food-processing plants. One of the few firms still making it is John Grant of Buncrana, in the north of Donegal. Apart from snuff the firm produces pipe tobacco, plug tobacco and tobacco for chewing. The latter is also gaining in popularity, particularly in America. It is said that taking tobacco in the form either of snuff or by chewing does not damage the lungs, unlike cigarette-smoking.

Snuff is made by grinding tobacco leaves, including the stems, until they are reduced to powder form. This grinding was originally done between a pair of vertical stones, but is now pulverised by hammers which break down the tobacco into fine grains. Grants produce five different flavours, among them high toast, pepper-mint, and menthol. The flavours are added to the dry powdered tobacco to form the snuff and the taste may also be varied by

Sorting tobacco for making snuff at Buncrana, Co. Donegal.

toasting it in a pan. Snuff has recently had excise duty lifted from it so that it is now relatively cheap. It is taken by placing a small amount on the hand and by sniffing it up into the nostrils. Formerly, as much tobacco was taken in the form of snuff as was smoked, and it was kept in richly decorated boxes much sought after by collectors. Gradually it fell out of favour but once again it is regaining some of its former popularity.

Stone-Ground Wheat

As so-called health foods have been gaining in popularity, a renewed interest is being taken in flour from wheat that has been ground between millstones, and this is being carried out at a mill belonging to Roscrea Abbey in Co. Tipperary, where there are two pairs of French burr stones. The stones are about four inches in

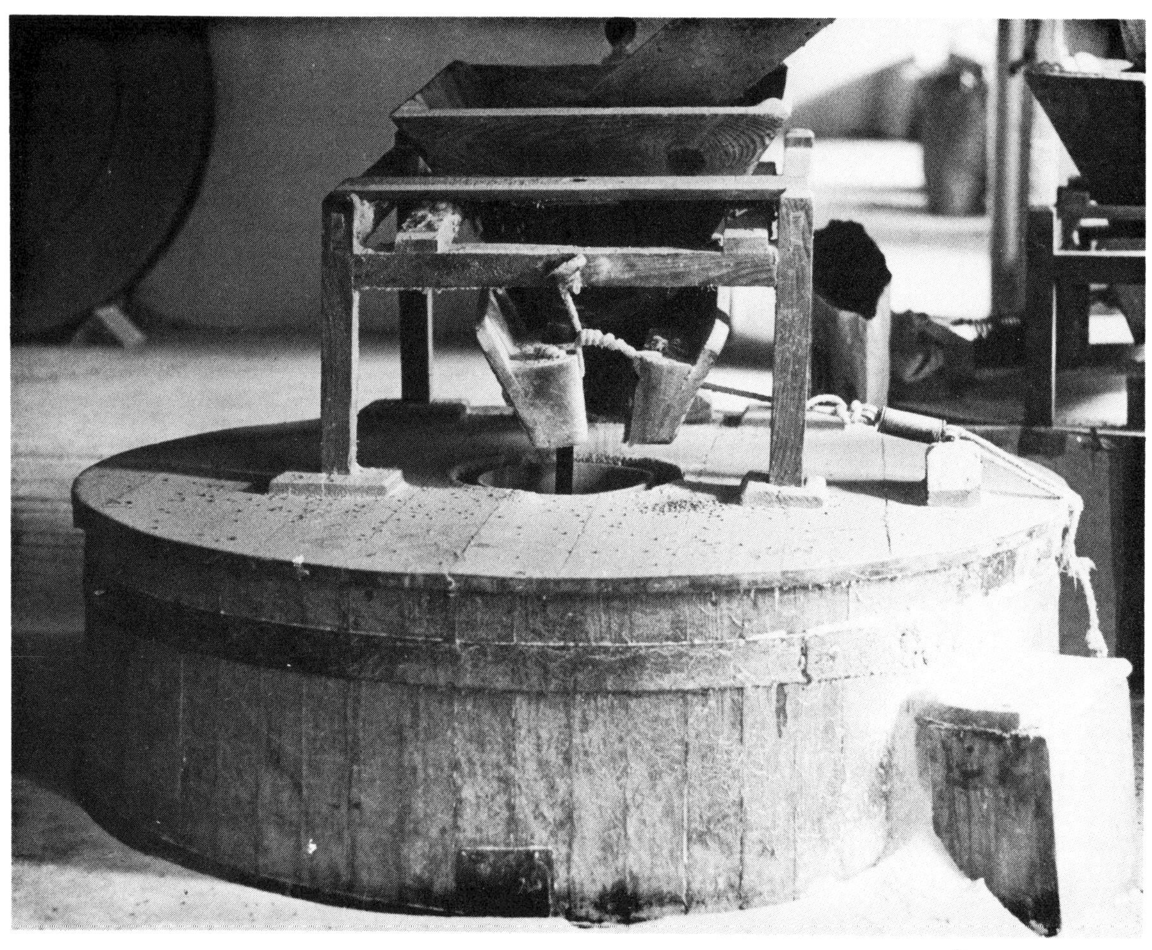

diameter, and in turn are composed of a number of stones bound tightly together and held by an iron band. It is very hard, with a number of grooves cut along the surface which shear the wheat. They have to be dressed every two years which means that a millwright has to re-cut or sharpen the cutting edges of the grooves

Milling stone ground flour at Roscrea, Co. Tipperary.

118

with a sharp metal mill bill. The bottom of the pair is called the 'bed stone' and remains stationery, while the upper one is the 'runner stone', and rotates. It used to be driven by water power but is now turned electrically. Grain is fed in automatically by a simple but effective mechanism, and enters through a hole in the centre of the runner stone. As it is ground it slowly works its way to the outside edge of the stones which are enclosed in a wooden case to prevent the flour dispersing. The latter comes out ground fine and quite hot, and drops through a pipe in the floor leading into a sack. For successful milling the moisture content of the wheat must be correct and the gap between the stones finely adjusted to obtain good-quality flour. The flour that emerges is wholemeal and contains all the wheat, including the germ. Nutrition experts consider it makes the finest possible bread.

Malting Barley

Malt is made from barley and is the main ingredient for making both whiskey and beer, so large amounts are needed. Its production is a specialised and scientific craft and is now mostly done in large tanks under strictly controlled conditions with the various operations mechanised as much as possible. However there remain a trio of what might be called old-fashioned malting floors under the traditional pagoda roofs, situated at Enniscorthy, Kilkenny and Ards. The grain for malting is specially grown, mostly of the emmer or ark royal variety, and is always spring sown because there is less risk of disease then than in autumn. Fortunately a large area of Ireland, with its temperate climate, is ideal for growing barley. The seed is invariably supplied by the malting firm to the farmers who grow it under contract with specific instructions about fertilising, since too much nitrogen may affect the taste of the beer.

To malt barley it is first steeped in a water tank for two days, then spread out on a large malting floor. It quickly starts to heat and germinate and must to be turned over at regular intervals with a special type of hand-drawn plough. After six days on the floor it begins to sprout and develop small rootlets. During this time the starch in the grain begins to turn to sugar, one of the vital ingredients for brewing, and at this critical stage it is transferred to a heating chamber under the pagoda roof and laid on a mesh floor. Fires are lit below and the heat dries the barley for about two days. The rootlets are removed to become high-protein cattle feed once the barley has become malted; in appearance the grains look normal but if bitten they have the characteristic malt taste.

Malting by this method requires a team of four or five who bring their experience to bear in regulating the temperature of the malting floor and turning the grain. They claim they make better malt than that produced by more modern methods, while the price of their produce remains about the same.

Whiskey

The crafts that go into the making of whiskey include the malting of the barley on the malting floors (see page 119), the making of the storage barrels by coopers (see page 87), and the coppersmith's work in the construction of the stills. Following the process through after malting, the malt is milled or ground, and then mashed by adding hot water to it in a large metal mash tun to form the wort. After several days it is drained off into huge wooden fermentation vats, magnificent examples of the cooper's art, which last for many decades. Yeast is then added and the wort ferments. When fermentation has ceased the resulting liquid is distilled in huge copper-pot stills. It is distilled three times, differing in this respect from Scotch whisky which is distilled twice. The liquid is

*The stills at the Old Bushmills
Distillery, Co. Antrim.*

distilled to about one tenth of its original volume, and it is then poured into the barrels where it matures for at least three years.

The earliest licence to distil was granted to 'Old Bushmills' distillery in 1608, whereas the first licence issued in Scotland was in 1824. In both countries illegal distilling had flourished for many years before these dates and is, of course, still continued today with the production of poteen, which is produced in a similar way to whiskey, but usually contains additives such as potatoes. The advent of calor gas enables it to be produced without the tell-tale blue smoke that used to arise from the remote areas where it was distilled.

Fishing Nets

A wide variety of nets are required by fishermen: drift nets, trammel nets, tangle nets for lobsters, seine nets, trawl nets and eel nets, among others. They are all now made from synthetic materials,

Working on fishing nets at Killybegs, Co. Donegal.

122

woven by large firms like Bridport Gundry and Cosalt. The industry is highly mechanised but machines generally only turn out a large flat piece of netting which in turn has to be fitted out by hand.

As an example a seventy-foot trawler might have £30,000 worth of nets and an annual repair bill of about a quarter of this amount. The life of a net is variable; it can be several years but can also be torn at any time by getting caught on an obstruction on the sea bed. Fitting out nets and major repairs are carried out in large lofts, usually with wooden floors and plenty of light, using special netting needles. There is room to hang up the nets or lay them out for inspection, and plenty of space in which to work. A lot of it is done by girls, and among places where such lofts are situated are Killybegs in Co. Donegal and Kilkeel in Co. Down.

Lacemaking

Until the eighteenth century there was a heavy demand for lace for items such as collars and cuffs and later for trimming underwear,

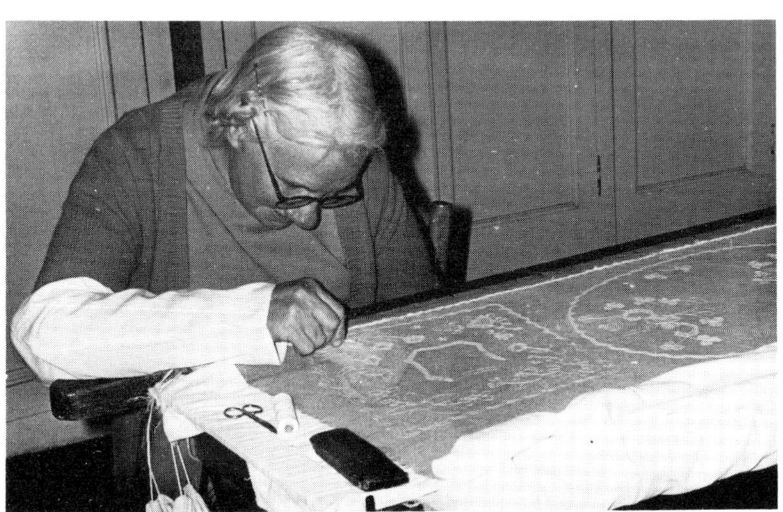

Making Limerick lace.

handkerchiefs and embellishing wedding veils and dresses. Ireland has a long tradition of lacemaking, where it was introduced by refugees fleeing from mainland Europe, though the craft was badly hit when lace began to be made by machinery in the middle of the nineteenth century. Today it is kept alive by convents and a few other individuals.

One famous centre is Limerick, where in the Convent of the Good Shepherd about ten women produce exquisitely fine work. Limerick lace was introduced to Ireland 150 years ago and its manufacture was once an important local industry. It is needle run superimposed on Brussels net with a six sided mesh. The net is fixed on frames which are placed over trestles giving a horizontal working surface. The pattern, drawn on material such as calico, is held or tacked under the net, and it is then outlined on it with a needle and very fine cotton. Having outlined the pattern the design is filled in using a number of different stitches, such as diamond and herring bone and the finished work is reversable, having the same pattern on both sides.

The other well known variety of Irish lace is called Carrick-macross. It was also introduced about 150 years ago from Italy and gained a good reputation before declining and being rescued and revived by Sisters of St Louis Convent at Carrickmacross, Co. Monaghan. Here it is a cottage industry, with designs and materials supplied by the convent, who market the completed articles. The work is painstaking and slow, and stocks cannot be built up, such is the demand.

Carrickmacross lace is slightly different from that of Limerick, although it is made on the same type of Brussels net either of cotton or nylon, while the stitching is of fine cotton. Extensive use is made of applique, in which pieces of organdie are cut out and stitched onto the design. Also embodied is guipure work, which consists of cutting out small pieces of the net and stitching around it. Special scissors are used for this, one of the points having a small

124

A sample of Carrickmacross lace.

metal bobble fixed on the end so it will not snag during the cutting process. A further difference is that the lace is not held in a frame but in the hand. The design is on paper backed with tissue, and is loosely tacked to the net with organdie applique on top.

Flax

Linen is woven from flax, which used to be an important crop supplying the mills around Belfast, although its cultivation has now almost entirely disappeared. Flax grows to a height of about three feet and is harvested after the pale blue flowers have fallen and before the seeds have formed. It is pulled by the root, which is slow, backbreaking work, and the crops tended to be grown in small areas so that the farming family could harvest it in the rather short time that it was ready. It was then bundled up into sheaves or beets ready for the next operation of retting and rotting. The beets were steeped in a flax dam, where they were held under water for a period of seven to twelve days. During this time the fibres separated from the outer casing and the core, giving off a foul smell in the process.

The flax was then dried and broken by rolling it with a heavy stone wheel. Afterwards came the scutching, done by hand, which suited the farming calendar as it could be done in winter. The flax was held by hand, placed over a wooden support and beaten with a wooden knife-shaped instrument which separated the fibres from the broken outer stalks, an operation subsequently carried out in a water-powered flax mill.

It was then spun into yarn ready for weaving, although when woven, the resulting linen cloth was a brown colour. Before the days of chemical bleaching, the cloth was laid out in fields to expose it to the sun. When sufficiently bleached it was ready for the final process of beetling, in which heavy wooden weights were dropped on to the cloth to thicken it and give an even finish and sheen.

There is a working beetling mill at Wellbrook, Co. Tyrone, which is preserved by the National Trust, and the Ulster Folk Museum at Cultra, Co. Down, has a flax mill, a watch hut from a bleaching green and a Jacquard loom set up to make the intricate patterns of linen damask.

Wooden Hurdles

Wooden hurdles are found lining the banks and channels leading to the eel traps on the River Bann between Lough Neagh and the north coast. They are made by interweaving willow rods, about one

Eel traps on the River Bann. Woven wooden hurdles are used to direct the flow of water.

inch in diameter, between vertical stakes in exactly the way sheep hurdles are made. They serve the dual purpose of protecting the river banks and guiding the eels through the channels where the traps are situated.

APPENDIX

Artist Craftsmen

Artist craftsmen have not generally been included in this book. They are now being encouraged and given tax advantages to move to the Irish Republic, with the result that many of them are not Irish-born. Notable exceptions are the Pearce family, with Simon Pearce achieving international fame as a glass-blower, and the rest of this family as potters. Waterford glass has been revived, and its glass-blowers and engravers, mostly local recruits, have also become known internationally for their skill. They may be seen plying their trade on a well-guided tour of the works. Craftsmen potters are also on the increase, as are some silversmiths and jewellers, to mention just a few of the wide variety of artist crafts being practised on an increasing scale.

Craft Displays

The following offer permanent craft displays and are open to the public:

Bunratty Castle and Folk Park, Co. Clare, has an interesting collection of thatched buildings where a number of craftsmen can be seen at work, including candlemakers and a farrier.

Craggaunowen, Co. Clare, has a number of buildings exhibiting aspects of thatching and dry stone walling.

Glencolumbkille, Co. Donegal, offers a collection of interesting thatched dwellings and traditional furniture.

Muckross House, near Killarney, has a crafts display, and craftsmen may sometimes be seen at work.

Ulster Folk and Transport Museum, Cultra, Co. Down, is an excellent museum with an extensive collection of cottages, plus a variety of other buildings which have been re-erected on site, and provides an authentic recreation of Ulster folk life and vernacular architecture.

Further Reading

The Craft Hunter's Pocket Guide and *Craftsmen of Ireland,* both published by Bord Failte, Dublin, list a wide variety of artist craftsmen, some of whom can be seen at work, while *A guide to Northern Ireland Crafts and Craftsmen* lists practitioners in Northern Ireland, and is available from the Local Enterprise Development Unit, Belfast. Other relevant publications include:

A Good Beginning: Setting Up and Running Your Own Craft Workshop, Crafts Council of Ireland, Dublin.

Irish Weaving, Spinning and Dyeing, Lillias Mitchell, Dun Dalgean Press, Dundalk.

Rush Cutting, Joan Norman, Crafts Council of Ireland, Dublin.

Weaving: The Irish Inheritance, EF Sutton, Gilbert Dalton, Dublin.